The End of Airports

WITHDRAWN
No longer the property of the
Boston Public Library.
Sale of this material benefits the Library.

D1127152

The End of Airports

Christopher Schaberg

Bloomsbury Academic
An imprint of Bloomsbury Publishing Inc

BLOOMSBURY
NEW YORK • LONDON • OXFORD • NEW DELHI • SYDNEY

Bloomsbury Academic
An imprint of Bloomsbury Publishing Inc

1385 Broadway
New York
NY 10018
USA

50 Bedford Square
London
WC1B 3DP
UK

www.bloomsbury.com

BLOOMSBURY and the Diana logo are trademarks of Bloomsbury Publishing Plc

First published 2016

© Christopher Schaberg, 2016

All rights reserved. No part of this publication may be reproduced or transmitted in any form or by any means, electronic or mechanical, including photocopying, recording, or any information storage or retrieval system, without prior permission in writing from the publishers.

No responsibility for loss caused to any individual or organization acting on or refraining from action as a result of the material in this publication can be accepted by Bloomsbury or the author.

Library of Congress Cataloging-in-Publication Data
Schaberg, Christopher.
The end of airports/Christopher Schaberg.
pages cm
Summary: "A sequel and companion to the groundbreaking The Textual Life of Airports, The End of Airports combines critical theory, cultural studies, and media studies to encourage readers to think differently about contemporary air travel"– Provided by publisher.
Includes bibliographical references and index.
ISBN 978-1-5013-0550-4 (hardback) – ISBN 978-1-5013-0549-8 (paperback)
1. Airports. I. Title.
HE9797.S33 2015
387.7–dc23
2015011085

ISBN: HB: 978-1-5013-0550-4
PB: 978-1-5013-0549-8
ePub: 978-1-5013-0551-1
ePDF: 978-1-5013-0552-8

Typeset by Deanta Global Publishing Services, Chennai, India
Printed and bound in the United States of America

For Lara

Contents

Acknowledgments

Thanks to Mark Yakich, Ian Bogost, Greg Keeler, Pam Houston, Kara Thompson, Caren Kaplan, Nathan Henne, Hillary Eklund, Laura Murphy, Tim Welsh, Tim Morton, and Jeffrey Jerome Cohen for intellectual camaraderie and ongoing friendship as I worked on this book. Thanks to Catalina Ayubi for letting me use the haunting photograph on the cover of the book. I'm grateful to my research assistant Erin Little, for her assistance assembling the bibliography and for helpful suggestions as I finished the manuscript.

Dean Maria Calzada, Melanie McKay and the Center for Faculty Innovation, John Biguenet, and the English department at Loyola provided key support for the completion of this book. A big thanks to my Loyola students in 2014 who took my "Interpreting Airports" seminars, who worked through these topics with me, and who provided me with insightful feedback and enthusiasm for the project: Victoria Cinnater, Stratton Day, Peter De Armas, Alana (extra credit) Demaske, Camille Didelot-Hearn, Mik Grantham, Julia Houha, Fionn Hunter-Green, Ana Colon Longo, Madeline Marva, Colin Mausler, Victoria Odom,

Dave Thomas, Jack Vanchiere, Aaron Walker, Oliva Wells, Tom Whelan, Micaela Adamo, J. T. Barbour, Ernesto Caro, Frank Convit, Quynh-Nhu Dang, Emily Edwards, Adam El-Khazindar, Gabrielle Gatto, Madeline Horta, Kameron Lopreore, Kaleigh Macchio, Devon Malone, Leigh Maloney, Alex Samples, Adam Stelly, Cristina Suarez, Django Szilagi, Christiana Van Bree, Alex Ward, and Bryan Whittington—thanks for being great students and generous readers.

Once again I am indebted to Haaris Naqvi at Bloomsbury for his constant guidance, support, and verve on the publishing end of things. Thanks to the three anonymous readers who provided me with astute reader reports, which greatly improved the book. Malcolm Harris and Erika Kerruish provided valuable editorial feedback on essays that helped sharpen my writing. Thanks to *The Atlantic*, *The Millions*, *Narrative*, *The New Inquiry*, *The New York Times*, and *Transformations*, for publishing earlier drafts of parts of this book. And thank you to Robert Appelbaum for inviting me to Uppsala, Sweden, to give a plenary talk on airports at the Nordic Association for English Studies 2013 conference "Places & Non-places," where this book started to come together in my mind.

Thanks to my parents Susann and Jim Schaberg for all kinds of support, especially during the summer months. Finally, thanks to my family—Lara, Julien, and Camille—for traveling with me, for filling our home with love and wonder, and for tolerating my predawn writing sprees.

"Why do we still have airports? Why are they called airports?"

DON DELILLO, *COSMOPOLIS*

Points of Departure

As I write this, I am on a small regional jet, in seat 3D, flying over Lake Michigan en route to Minneapolis, where I will board another plane and fly to Bozeman, Montana. I am headed to Bozeman to visit the airport that I worked at over ten years ago. I worked there to supplement my income as a graduate student English instructor at Montana State University. At the time I wasn't thinking about the airport as a site of rich philosophical inquiry. I was just working there. Many years later, I started to recall the strange and routine parts of my airport work, and I realized I needed to get back, to see this space again.

What do I expect to find at this airport? Ostensibly I am returning to see how the small airport has changed over the past decade: how it has expanded, and how it has embraced (or not) the rise in digital technologies and the attendant pressures they put on air travel. In fact, though, I could discover most of these things by simply reading online about the airport's new amenities, features, and developments; I could look at the airport via satellite imagery, as I have done from time to time, to see how it has grown physically since I worked there—a new jet bridge here, a freshly paved parking lot there, new rooflines nearly matching the old ones.

But I am after something else—something more abstract, less concrete. Or maybe I'm after something *more* concrete, something ingrained in the mundane fabric and materials of the airport. I want to experience—or reexperience—life on the ground, at the airport.

I don't expect to find any of my old coworkers; my hunch is that they have all moved on, either to more illustrious airline careers (I heard a rumor that my former manager moved on to become an operations manager in Denver) or on to other jobs, other places, other lives—or even death. Neither do I expect to find stunning architecture or mind-bending art installations. Airport art tends toward the bland and innocuous—most of the time, anyway. No, I am after something more ambient, something happenstance and easily overlooked. I am after the end of airports.

Looking back, it was at the Bozeman airport that I began to take note of the oddities that I would go on to research and write about in a book called *The Textual Life of Airports: Reading the Culture of Flight* (first published in 2011). That book was about airports in American literature and popular culture: I analyzed how airports appear in poems, novels, advertisements, films, songs . . . and I traced the patterns that these appearances made. I explored American airports in and as texts: how these spaces show up in American literature, and how the airports themselves become open to interpretation. I offered nine theories for how airports could be understood as narrative devices in American culture.

The book you are holding in your hands is different. It is less a study of airport representations. It's more personal, a story of my own encounters with airports—both as actual places and as things to think about, as topics encountered in everyday life, such as in magazines and news feeds. It is thus a constrained book, idiosyncratic and verging on something close to autobiography at times. Yet this book is also expansive, and is about wide-reaching tensions, contradictions, and general feelings that haunt the experience of flight in the early twenty-first century.

As I was working on this book, people would inevitably ask me what I meant by "the end of airports." The title of this book refers to the end of airports as romantic places; the end of airports as sites of excitement; the end of airports as apexes of travel culture. The end of airports means the end of our ability to appreciate airports, to inhabit them as dynamic, fascinating, forward-looking spaces.

Certainly some people still experience airports as exciting and romantic. But for the vast majority of travelers (not to mention airline employees), airports are grim, decidedly unromantic realms—zones where we are subjected to screening, scrutiny, alienated labor, and inhumane treatment. It is this widespread, dispersed aura of gloom that, to me, portends the end of airports.

The end of airports also has to do with our everyday digital technologies—especially the ones in our pockets—that so radically outmode and outpace (even as they coexist with) the routines and rhythms of air travel. Simply consider the bumbling, at times chaotic, boarding procedures and departure operations that occur at an airport while at the same time passengers quietly use their smart phones to communicate and connect instantaneously at the delicate and precise taps of their thumbs. It's incredible to me that these two phenomena exist in the same historical moment: the slim lines of digital media, and the herding of bodies into airborne, dented metal tubes. Then again, iPhone screens crack, and thumbs get chewed. And a new plane is still something to see.

Some airports really do end; occasionally, airports are replaced by upgraded facilities; this is on the horizon in my own hometown of New Orleans as I finish this book. And it is very likely that another form of travel will replace airports entirely, sometime in the not too distant future. It's hardly a sustainable mode of travel—it has a threshold, one that we may have already crossed.

We often refer to a golden age of air travel: it existed somewhere after the middle of the last century, perhaps, but definitively it is a time that has *passed*, is here no longer. Then there was what we might call an age of airport resignation: for several decades, humans have been resigned to a relatively static experience of air travel. In this period, we didn't ask for too much: just to get from origin to destination with minimal interruptions, but expecting the process to be a hassle all the same. The airport stands here as a place whose mere mention triggers reflexive eye rolling. We are still in this period, in many ways.

But there are fault lines and stress points that suggest a dawning new era of air travel. Increasingly, in airports you can see most clearly the signs of this new epoch, its instantiated paradoxes (here/nowhere, passivity/rage) and exasperating everyday demands: assisted self–check-in, complicated fee structures, tiers of boarding, jammed overhead bins for carry-ons.... The strangest thing might be that it doesn't look that much different than it did ten, twenty years ago. Yet even though airliners are essentially the same as they have been for around fifty years, something has changed, *is* changing. And partly what is changing is that there is no promise of change, only a sort of numb acceptance of the beleaguered experience of flight. This acceptance is often signaled and mediated by where we look in airports: down into our palms, where faster and quieter machines connect us to one another. The end of airports is the age of smart phones.

Running along the bottom of the pages of this book are aphorisms: pithy, occasionally enigmatic statements and observations about airports. They are at turns playful and serious; they are also acts of adaptation and pastiche. Some of the sources of the aphorisms may be vaguely recognizable or blatantly obvious; others will be more cryptic, harder to track down. They are all true.

These aphorisms are an attempt to spark concentrated thinking about airports—and also to highlight ways that literary and philosophical writing can be harnessed to think through airports, even when the original passage's topic was perhaps far afield. These paratexts can be played like little games: you can try to discover who I am channeling at each turn. Or, you can simply read them and ruminate on their meanings, without the need for any firm origin or destination.

I started to experiment with this form when I began using the microblogging service Twitter, and I was challenged and amazed by how words—and slogans, and ideas, and whole understandings of the world—could be crunched into 140 characters. In this book I have taken these ephemeral digital missives and repurposed them for print, for slow reading.

Twitter offered other avenues of thinking for the development of this book. If you conduct a search using the hashtag *#airport* on Twitter, you gain access to a continually running stream of tiny messages that reflect an incredible diversity of airport impressions. Consider this note of surprise by @vaniped:

> Comfort seats while waiting for our flight. Cool. #amsterdam #airport http://instagr.am/p/K4RYuYiLpE/

The surprised dispatch links to an Instagram snapshot of said seats. Or contemplate this more succinct observation by @AngelaSimmons:

> Super. Bored. #Airport http://mob.li/_PNRoP

In this case, the linked text offers something just out of reach—tantalizing yet inaccessible unless you have an application called "Mobli." But even without the app, even without knowing what exactly @AngelaSimmons has captured, the scathing indictment is clear: the airport has resulted in stalled time, and someone perhaps known as Angela Simmons communicates this attitude in two words punctuated by periods, as if to re-mark the spacing of time.

Of course, there's nothing all that unique about the hashtag for airports. This is what Twitter *does*: it records millions upon millions of thoughts, impressions, reactions, conversations, and sensations that course through the digitally networked parts of the planet, minute by minute. Still there's something about watching the airport tweets unfold, and noticing how they range from enchanted to disgusted, from poetic to pragmatic. As a catalog of ambivalent experiences and heightened emotional states, *#airport* is an apt point of departure for this book.

There is something peculiar about the ways that social media intersect with airports, and this is one of the things I puzzle over in the following pages. To put it simply, as more and more humans take journeys (or "connect") via mobile devices and personal computers, these smaller-scale technologies may end up trumping actual flight.

So much of this book is about the coexistence and collisions of what we rather sloppily designate as old and new media. I have thought a lot about how digital communications outpace—while nevertheless nestling into—the more sluggish and clunky enterprise of modern flight. Even when things go utterly smooth, as they are right this instant, as I cruise 30,000 feet above Wisconsin, the tail-mounted engines roar feverishly and I hear the galley trolley banging into seats as our flight attendant Kara, scarf askew, shuttles it down the aisle offering precariously filled cups of coffee and diminutive bags of pretzels.

The tenuousness of human flight is inescapable, and it is foregrounded by the sleekness of our mobile communications. When I see the Passbook prompt for me to "Fly Delta Today at 7:35" flash across my iPhone screen, inviting me to simply swipe my thumb in order to access my virtual boarding pass, the thought passes through my head, *If only it were so easy to fly*. For I know the matrix of factors, contingencies, and personalities that await me at the airport. And I know that what my iPhone is really driving at is the end of airports.

In this book I treat airports as a dispersed yet also paradoxically concentrated matter of contemporary everyday life. Airports are no longer simply places of exception, or privilege, or exclusion; they take on a displaced quality, popping up in weird ways in unexpected places. So we have the Twitter hashtag *#airport*, which scrambles various geographical points, semantic outbursts, and lines of transit across the digital networks, into our pockets and before our eyes.

And as I finish writing this introduction, I am no longer in an airplane, nor am I in an airport. I'm in my small house in New Orleans, sitting at my dining table. It's 3:28 a.m., and I'm listening to the eerie night noises that echo up from the loading docks on the Mississippi River, a few blocks away. And yet, via Twitter, I can be momentarily transported into people's airport adventures, disseminated around the globe. And to make matters more curious, the way I tap in to other people's trips is by turning on the metaphorically named device "AirPort." Airports are everywhere, and they are increasingly hard to pin down.

But I'm getting ahead of myself; airports are also just airports, just places where we go to board airplanes and send our luggage along on parallel (if largely invisible) paths. And the truth is that I like to travel, and I find airports intriguing on so many levels—I *like* to think about them, and to write about them. This is not to say that I never experience airports as soul-crushingly boring or absurdly regimented; who doesn't, sometimes—or maybe even most of the time?

I live about 1,200 miles from where I grew up, and so I tend to fly to visit family at least once a year. And then there are academic conferences, which I fly to from time to time, once or twice a year. But I am hardly a frequent flier; I'm not active on flier forums concerning airport amenities and airliner seating configurations; I do not have elite status on a major airline. If I write with some unique insight into the world of air travel, it comes more from my time working for an airline, making my daily rounds and becoming familiar with the ins and outs of airport life. My insights also emerge from my scholarly interests in space, place, and environment: I am always curious how airports mediate their place in space, and how they are situated in relation to their regions and surrounding ecosystems. This is all to say that I am writing from a hybrid perspective: from the standpoint of a former airport worker *and* from the viewpoint of an ordinary traveler. This is hardly a manifesto for the last redoubt of civility remaining in First Class. (Quite the contrary.) Yet I am not necessarily hastening or sullenly foreshadowing the end of air travel in this book, either. Rather, I am documenting what I see to be some of the paradoxes and contradictory sentiments that are present in airports, and that, to me, suggest that the epoch of human flight might be gradually coming to a close.

Perhaps airports are simply no more than strange spaces—and in that case all I am noticing are the *ends* of airports, or just how they function on a normal basis. For the word "end" can mean the final part of something (or its death), but it can also mean something's object or purpose, or even the point when something *begins*—such as when we invoke the phrase "in the end" to mean that a decision has to be made, a course needs to be taken. Curiously, we often say "in the end" just to underscore the fact that things are ongoing. What follows, then, is a series of perceived hints and indefinite glimpses of the end of airports. This book is not an obituary; it's more like a mystery. What is this elaborate system we've devised and made relatively uniform around the globe? How does it feel to be a part of it? Where are its frayed ends?

This book not only moves forward from my first book about airports, it also goes back in time. In order to show you how I've come to think about the end of airports, I have to back up and show you how I got here. The first part of this book, called "Work," recounts my experiences as an airline employee between the years 2001 and 2003 at the small airport outside Bozeman.

The second part of the book is called "Travel." I'm using this term not only to refer to my own travels to and around various airports, but also to suggest the conceptual wiggle room that these structures involve: airports mean so many things, from boredom to romance, from high adventure to the daily grind. Airports *travel*; they are incredibly flexible in terms of how they mesh with and get insinuated into everyday life beyond the proper bounds of the airfield. This part of the book is an assortment of travels—paths of inquiry—around a range of objects that prop up and riddle air travel and its myriad modalities.

Throughout this book you'll find that my attitude toward airports is very mixed. I find them fascinating and compelling as anthropological sites; I also find them deeply vexing and troubling in terms of what they say about how we have come to inhabit this planet, and how we migrate.

My hope is that this book sparks contemplative reflection and critical awareness around the topic of airports. The culture of flight is full of oddities and niceties that are open to observation and wonder—and potentially to revision.

Part One

Work

Cross-Utilized Agent

A long frontage road runs from the town of Bozeman, Montana, to the airport eight miles away in Belgrade. The Bridger Mountains trail off on the northern horizon—bulging humps of gray and dark green that rise up off the valley floor.

It was a March morning in 2001, and I was driving out to the airport—not to fly, but to apply for a job. The newspaper ad bore the old logo of United Airlines, and the position title was "cross-utilized agent." I parked my old Volkswagen Jetta in the short-term parking lot and strolled across the lot to the curbside sliding doors. This was an odd sensation: to arrive at the airport with no intention of going anywhere.

I have always liked to fly. I feel a weirdly sustained high when checking in for a flight, waiting to board, and watching the ground fall away during takeoff. So the thought of working at an airport was exhilarating—I would get to see what happens behind the scenes.

As I entered the controlled environment of the terminal, I spotted the United sign and walked up to the counter. There were no passengers in the check-in area; Muzak floated down from speakers somewhere above: an instrumental rendition of the Beatles's "Norwegian Wood." When I asked for a job application, the crisply uniformed agent at the United Airlines

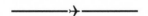

Airports are a substitute for the legends that used to open up space to something different.

desk looked at me skeptically. (I had a scruffy beard and a ponytail at the time.)

That afternoon, I went to a hole-in-the-wall barbershop on Main Street in Bozeman, and had my hair cut short and neat. I trimmed my beard considerably. When I drove out to the airport the next day to submit my completed application, the same agent gave me a curt nod of approval as he took my application and turned toward the backroom.

I was called in for a group interview at the airport later that week. The interview took place in a strangely corporatized conference room in a nether region of the terminal; I had never realized that airports had rooms not dedicated to the primary act of flight. This would be the first of many lessons in opening up the space of airports, seeing them in so many different ways, beyond simple corridors for travel.

In the conference room, I sat around a long table with a dozen or so other applicants, each of us touting our qualifications. It was surprisingly grueling, and at times very embarrassing; we were a mixed bag of locals and bright-eyed wanderers, youngsters and old-timers . . . all here vying for a part-time position (no benefits to speak of) that started at $7.25 an hour.

That evening I got a phone call inviting me for a follow-up interview the following day. This time, it was just the manager Lance, the supervisor Brad, and myself. Lance's office was small

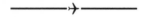

Roughly speaking: airports are colorless.

but his model airliners, angled slightly up, looked impressive on his top shelf.

Two days later, to my excitement, I was hired to work part-time for SkyWest Airlines, a small regional carrier that flew under the livery of United Express. SkyWest operated two Canadair Regional Jets (CRJs) that flew from Santa Barbara to Denver, and from Denver to Bozeman—and then back, three times a day. We loaded and unloaded these planes, kept them clean between flights (and overnight), and issued last-minute tickets and refunds to travelers.

By late 2014, SkyWest planes would be servicing 186 destinations under a variety of airline logos, and operating over 300 CRJs. During the time I worked for SkyWest, I witnessed the ramping up of a trend toward regional aircraft: a shift from Boeing 737 and Airbus 319/320 (100 –150+ passenger airliners) that rarely filled to capacity on short domestic routes, in favor of the 50–to-90-seat jets that the airlines could fill up with passengers—and thus, with revenue. (This trend has since been curbed, as regional airports have closed or been developed, and as airlines have merged and fleets have been reshuffled.)

One of the parts of my initial job training—a long week spent in a drab office complex somewhere in downtown Salt Lake City—involved memorizing innumerable three-letter airport codes around the country. There was my station, BZN;

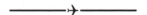

———✈———

Airports keep us from thinking precisely about the ambiguity of nature.

and then there was ORD, ATL, DFW, GRR, DTW, MSP, DEN, LGA, MIA, SMF, MSY, JFK, SFO, OAK, LAX, SEA, PDX, TVC, PHX, PSP, SBA . . . . The list goes on and on, and these codes still pop up in my mind at random intervals—little fragments of geographic identifiers running through my brain, less related to a map than to the memory of baggage tag aesthetics. In Salt Lake City (SLC), I watched videos about how to move around planes without scratching the wings or getting decapitated, and I was given a thick three-ring binder full of safety tips and awkward acronyms, airline slogans and corporate ideals, and pages of codes for hazardous materials that might be transported on any given day.

When I returned to Bozeman I was officially a cross-utilized agent. This meant that I not only checked in passengers for their flights and boarded them at the gate; I also handled baggage, deiced the aircraft when it was freezing, cleaned planes at night, and maintained all the auxiliary vehicles—from the "belt-loader" baggage conveyor to the squat "TUG" tractor used to haul around baggage carts, from the loud external generator to the simple lavatory reservoir on wheels, feces slopping in an internal blue bath. (Employees who work these parts of the job, hustling around outside and on the ground, are often called "rampers.") I was immersed in all the processes that I had watched take place outside so many window seats. These machines and actions were

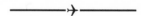

The task is on some level to forget about the arrangement of planes on the tarmac and instead focus on our experience of smaller-scale matters.

no longer esoteric or exotic looking—they simply comprised my workplace.

Checking In

Not long ago, checking in for flights was still a complex social interaction. You would go to the airport and line up with other people, some of whom you might see on your flight. Likewise, the airline agents would administer the experience for all, issuing boarding passes, printing baggage tags, and looking into possible upgrades. All while making conversation, fielding queries, and occasionally being the venting points for prior flight debacles.

With the bloom of online services, smart phones, and the proliferation of automated check-in kiosks at airports, the practice of checking in has become more dispersed and self-managed, and less social. Checking in is now one of those myriad modern practices that invite people to pay for something, and then to do tasks that used to involve paid labor: the work of checking in for a flight, selecting seats, and printing boarding passes has been moved away from the compensated airline employee at the airport, and is now part of the common traveler's home office experience, even mobilized for maximum efficiency. In other words, we now not only pay for a ticket, but also do many of the

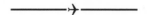

It may be deemed almost superfluous to establish the fact that, among people at large, the business of airports is not about going anywhere.

minor tasks that used to require airline employees. Some might celebrate this as putting the power into the hands of the people. Nevertheless, passengers are now doing for free (however clumsily or smoothly) what others used to be trained and paid to do.

When I worked at the airport, there was still the mystique of the real ticketing agent. I mastered the comportment of the fickle airline employee, leaning exaggeratedly into the counter and propping one foot up on the metal bar that ran about six inches off the floor. My blue-striped, collared United shirt signaled specialized knowledge and privileged information. The mat under my feet was one of those gel-filled cushions made for the type of work that requires long stretches of standing in one spot.

In those days, check-in began exactly two hours before the flight. I learned how to be fiercely oblivious to passengers who were itching to check in before the two-hour mark. I knew how to tilt my head at a certain angle, furrow my brow, and stare deeply into the computer monitor, clicking the keyboard occasionally, while passengers too early to check in stood in line before me trying to make unsubtle sounds in their throats and crinkle their itinerary papers so as to grab my attention.

While standing there, sometimes I used the time to read the United Airlines weekly briefing; there was a quiz to do upon completion, and our collective scores were sent to our managers. If I had already finished this task, it was still policy not to

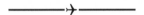

Yet this is a paradoxical discovery: for airports, which so effectively discredit other versions of travel, also cause people to walk great distances.

begin checking in passengers before two hours—I would find something else to do, like scanning what flights were delayed across the country, and for what alleged reasons.

At two hours before the flight—not a second before—I would look up with a bright smile and say, "Checking in for the flight to Denver?"

Seatback Pockets

The air hung heavy above the taxiway, sweltering hot in the summer, and moist with the mists of propylene glycol deicing fluid in the winter. And always, that ubiquitous burned aroma of jet engine exhaust.

While working at the airport, my hands grew calloused and raw from handling luggage, and the panoramic views consisted of either (A) the sliding doors leading out to the short-term parking lot or (B) a dull gray swath of concrete and asphalt leading out to the fenced perimeter of the airfield. The mountain peaks of the Bridger Range seemed to hover far in the background, a disjunctive wilderness that floated above my gritty workspace, layered like an *ukiyo-e* print.

My least favorite job at the airport was cleaning out the seatback pockets each night. After the last arrival, sometime between 10:00 p.m. and 1:00 a.m., depending on the weather

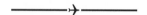

When does the airport become what it is? It presupposes the existence of another airport, somewhere.

in Denver, the aircraft spent the night in Bozeman, and part of my job was to thoroughly clean the plane before the end of my shift. The easy part, believe it or not, was the lavatory: It's such a wonderfully small space, and all covered with smooth plastic and elegant curves. You could spray all the surfaces with a generic and powerfully smelling cleaner, and wipe down every inch of the space in a few minutes, leaving the mini toilet, mini sink, mini mirror, and mini floor sparkling.

Even dumping the lavatory's actual contents from a slot on the exterior of the plane was clever and almost fun. You would snap on some big black rubber gloves, hook up a big black tube, unlock the valve, and coax all the solid matter and accompanying "blue juice" into a low-profile reservoir on wheels—the "lav cart." I only splashed shit on myself a few times, and when clumps of fecal matter are bright blue, somehow it all seems okay.

But then, at a certain point, I had to go back inside the plane and face the fifty seatback pockets. The seatback pockets on the new CRJ aircraft at the turn of the century were particularly vexing, because the elastic bands at the top of the pockets were very tight, still fresh from the factory, and this made it awkward to wedge an entire hand in, in order to clean out the trash. And you'd never know what the trash would consist of.

Good seatback pockets might house a folded magazine, a gum wrapper, or the crumpled stub of a boarding pass. Bad

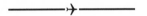

There is nothing dirty about airports, unless you are stuck inside one.

seatback pockets would contain the actual gum, puddles of Pepsi, crushed Crystal Geyser water bottles impossibly wedged in the bottom, an exploded pen wrapped in an inky napkin, congealed mini pretzels or cheddar-ranch crackers, gobs of snot caked on indecipherable other matter, or the razor edge of an uncrumpled boarding pass. Boarding passes could paper-cut to the bone; I have scars on my knuckles to prove it.

Before my airport job, I believed that the wilderness was a far-off place, located somewhere in the mountains or off in the desert. After working at the airport, I started to think of air travel itself as a kind of wilderness zone. Like an isolated butte or a forest with dense undergrowth, seatback pockets became one of the natural features I learned to navigate, and to maneuver with precision and attention to detail. Each enclosure had its own topography, with its own smell, texture, and mystery.

These days when I fly, my right hand instinctively makes the precise cupping shape I perfected to swipe out seatback pockets, moving from seat to seat to seat, across the aisle, back and forth, as so many midnight hours of my life passed by.

Pictures

When I worked at the airport, I was constantly looking off at the mountains, watching them change colors as I waited on the

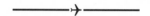

Objection, evasion, joyous distrust, and love of irony are signs of being at the airport.

tarmac for our United Express planes to land. On clear days I would look out toward the East and watch the little landing light blip on when the CRJ began its descent, 30 miles or so away. The severe landscape of the runway and taxiways seemed juxtaposed oddly against craggy peaks and lines of pines. The romance was everywhere in this landscape, all around—but always falling through the cracks, too—running away, as it were, like the viscous deicing fluid into the drainage ditches at the edge of the airfield. Wildness everywhere and vanishing, at once.

One month I took a camera to the airport whenever I worked, and I took pictures between flights. My girlfriend at the time had an old Nikon SLR camera, and I was learning to use it. I would drive the TUG around the tarmac, out toward the runway as far as I dared without being too conspicuously aimless, and then I would turn around abruptly and raise the camera. I'd frame the airport with a dramatic Delta Boeing 737 parked at its gate; or I would get right in front of the United Express CRJ and fill the entire picture with the nose of the plane, mountains just barely leaking into the frame. I would take four shots as a Northwest A319 took off, gaining speed then arcing up, leaving the mountains on the ground. I would later line these photos up as a sort of sequential panorama. I used up a dozen rolls of film that month, and sent each roll

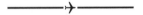

Presented with an airport you have never seen before, you can anticipate its texture.

off to Clark photo labs to be developed and sent back to me in 3-by-5 format, matte finish.

When the chubby packets would arrive back to me in the mail, I would always be vaguely let down. The views did not translate: the planes looked drab and uninteresting in pictures. One of the only pictures I ever liked was of the TUG I drove around, my primary work vehicle. It was a simple still life, somehow true to the thing (Plate 1). It is the standard compact diesel tractor that you see airline workers driving around the tarmac, pulling snakes of baggage carts and other miscellaneous utility trailers around aircraft. These were strange vehicles to drive, with their combination of powerful engines and slow speeds. There was a certain thrill in the way that these small machines could turn on a dime and pull long chains of baggage carts in tight loops; but there was also the low-grade disappointment that they could only go so fast, and the metal bar across your lower back was hardly comfortable for longer rides across the tarmac. There was something particularly disjunctive about the way the TUG looked against the mountains and the evening sky, all white and black and fierce geometry. This sort of captures how I've come to think about airports, as curious spaces that blot out whatever region you are in, even as airports must insist on regional value—the ability to differentiate place A from place B, and the need to travel between them.

All airports work us over completely.

Slow speed, powerful engine. This turns out to be an apt combination for thinking about the culture of flight: moving slowly, with the feeling of immense yet limited power, working unendingly and cyclically within defined boundaries—and hauling so much baggage.

Looking at the old picture I took of the TUG in Bozeman, scanned and illuminated on my slim MacBook Air screen, my metaphoric AirPort picking up the wireless DSL signal in my house, the scene seems almost quaint: the severe tarmac and a loud, powerful machine to move heavy cargo around. But of course, at some point my newly manufactured computer was loaded onto a trailer in another country, and hauled into the belly of a plane in order to arrive where it is, aglow in front of me now. So much of this book is about me trying to process how I looked at airports then, and how I look at them now—and how I look at myself looking at airports then, now.

There was another picture that had potential: it was of a Delta Connection CRJ that had just landed, and the ramp workers were servicing it in a hurry to prepare it for its next flight. They had tossed some bulging garbage bags on the baggage belt-loader, and their lumpy shapes looked startlingly similar to the clouds above the Olympics-themed livery on the jet, which depicted abstract mountains that were supposed to suggest Salt Lake City, also then weirdly mimicking the Bridger Mountains in the

In the new airport we recognize the old game, the habit of ignoring the facts and accepting a secondhand spectacle.

distance. It's a play of odd surface encounters between earth and sky, trash and technology.

Curiously, I never took any pictures of the airport's gritty interior. None of the eternal return of the baggage claim, none of the check-in area or the departure gates. Maybe I was too enamored with what lay outside, the layers of geology and technology I saw through the viewfinder. Or maybe this was only because I did not have a flashbulb for the camera, and it didn't take very good inside shots.

I turned a few of the photos into notecards that I sent to family and friends over the years. What remains is a pile of warped photos: the blurry ones, the odd ones, and the ones barely discernible in terms of subject/object. Looking at these photos now, I see my own golden age of flight: I was working for a young regional air carrier that was growing rapidly and had brand-new planes. The CRJs were freshly painted and smelled crisp, fresh off the assembly line, when you stepped aboard them. I must have liked the way that the shiny planes gleamed against the ruddy mountains in the background. Some pictures have shadowy baggage carts and boarding gates looming in the foreground, obfuscating the landscape or framing it—I'm not entirely sure which.

I have one fuzzy picture of the back of the airport, where the SkyWest station was located. I'm not even sure what to call this little place: An office? A garage? An operations center? In any

Human maturity consists of finding again the playfulness that one had as a child, in airports.

case, you can see two TUGs and the belt-loader, and a shadowy room in which two baggage carts sit, waiting for the next flight, to be loaded with luggage and hauled out to the aircraft. There is something vaguely apocalyptic about the picture: here we are on the tarmac of a twenty-first-century airport in the United States, and there are no people around. No faces in the windows, no profiles with roller bags angled at full tilt, no coveralled workers dutifully maintaining the vehicles. It's like the end of airports.

In another picture, I'm behind the SkyWest TUGs, and I have caught a Northwest DC-9 taxiing routinely toward the runway (Plate 2). It is strange to me that Northwest has now been phased out entirely, having been absorbed by Delta. I Google the airline, and see how Northwest exists now as a historical curiosity, details delineated and debated by aviation geeks on Wikipedia. Northwest apparently began painting its planes' tails red during the Second World War, when it was flying military equipment and personnel to Alaska for the war effort; the red tails were more visible in the hard weather conditions of Alaska.

As I read about Northwest and its fairly elaborate history of mergers and acquisitions, I am struck by a linked phrase: the "Airbus A320 family." If I were to click on this link, surely it would take me to the appropriate Wikipedia page that provides the history, incidents, and design specs of the aircraft. But I don't follow that link. Instead, I linger on the idea of aircraft as *families*.

———✈———

The next step in the development of airports is to bring out the particular conditions of their coexistence with other places.

Was I seeing something along these lines in my photos of aircraft on the runways and taxiways of the Bozeman airport? These aircraft, even the ones of different makes and airlines, were all part of the same family, my family, as they landed and departed out of this little town in Montana in the first part of the twenty-first century.

I took so many pictures of planes being unloaded and loaded, with silly baggage carts strewn about and scuffed orange cones placed on the tarmac at the nose, wings, and tail of the aircraft. What did I see in these images? What was I trying to capture? They are utterly unremarkable pictures. And yet, to me this was art, somehow. How else do I explain this pile of arguably monotonous photos sitting here in front of me, thirteen years later? It's like a family photo album, charting the relations of a cyborg family of animals, machines, and buildings.

Meal Kits

SkyWest used to give little meal kits in colorful cardboard boxes to its passengers on the flights from Santa Barbara to Denver and from Denver to Bozeman.

At the end of each day, we cross-utilized agents would clean out the extra meal kits and stack them in our office refrigerator—there, they were up for grabs. I would sometimes arrive to work

It is quite obvious that the airport is neither good nor evil, let alone the best of all or worst of all places.

very hungry, and wolf down three or four meal kits before starting my shift. The breakfast kits included a firm banana, a plain bagel, a plastic tub of cream cheese, and a packet of fruit spread. The lunch kits included a ham and cheese croissant sandwich, one pouch of Dijonnaise, a small bag of Fritos, and a cellophane-wrapped cookie. I can still conjure the predictable taste of each of these items, their particular flavors enhanced or maybe muted—I'm not sure which—after having sat in the compressed air of a jet aircraft for a day, hugged tightly by plastic wrap.

The other free ration at the airport was the standard airline snack-mix. Here I am referring to those miniature silvery bags that contain indeterminate conglomerates of cheddar-and-ranch dusted crackers, pretzel twists, bagel chips, and/or tortilla triangles. The contents are best consumed in a single open-bag lift to the mouth, and gobbled up in one not-so-enormous bite. After six or seven bags, I was usually full enough to go unload a plane full of luggage, or to deice the aircraft before takeoff. We had boxes and boxes of these little bags of snack-mix. Even as they changed themes, names, and ingredients over time, they all seemed to come from Solon, Ohio. I often wondered about that factory in Solon, what it would be like to work there. For instance, did the snack-mix workers eat the snack-mix on their breaks? Did the snack-mix workers get to take the factory rejects

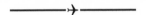

In a well-kept airport no matter how simple or how economical it is, people should be only too grateful to take their share of the everyday.

home for their kids to eat? What did the factory rejects look like? How long could you live on snack-mix alone?

A couple of months into the job, I was flown to Seattle for several weeks to learn the United Airlines computer and ticketing system. The lessons were taught in a windowless basement room in an office park near the SEA-TAC airport. The lessons went on all day: how to check flight schedules, how to assemble an itinerary, how to book a reservation, how to change a reservation, how to cancel a reservation, how to issue flight credits for cancelations due to mechanical problems, and so on. I learned that masterful technique of clicking robotically away at a keyboard while saying things like "Hmmm . . . well . . . I'm sorry, but it doesn't look like there are any available flights to your destination until next Tuesday. But let's check some other options . . ."

I remember taking the bus into downtown Seattle a few of those afternoons, and eating smoked salmon at the Pike Place Market. But aside from a vague memory of an office park cafeteria, and the taste of sour concentrated orange juice, I have little recollection of what else I ate during those long training days in Seattle, between those hours spent in the dark basement room staring at a blue screen, making hypothetical reservations for imaginary people, sending no planes anywhere, not yet, but getting ready to.

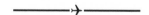

The real efforts of airports are necessarily discreet, dispersed, and almost imperceptible.

Soon after I returned to Bozeman, the meal kits were discontinued. The last few meal kits in our refrigerator were consumed unceremoniously, the sprightly boxes crumpled up and discarded, as if gone forever.

Tetris

I often thought of loading baggage as a game of human-scale Tetris. Each fifty-passenger flight that I worked would usually require two standard-size luggage carts full of roller bags, snowboard carriers, ski bags, Pelican cases, octagonal metal film canisters, long cylindrical fishing rod holders, and hard-sided suitcases. Occasionally there would be a kayak, or a casket.

The tail cargo section of the CRJ is roughly six feet wide by six feet deep by six feet tall at the apex. On any normal day, I would have about ten minutes in which to load the objects in such a way that (A) they all fit, (B) nothing was squashed, and (C) the load would not cascade dangerously onto the baggage handler on the other end, upon the flight's arrival.

There are different styles that baggage handlers adopt. These include (1) hard-sided suitcases, flat, all across the bottom, and build up from there; (2) large roller bags lined vertically on their sides along the back wall, followed by duffel bags and then ski

The classic demonstration of a space without structure is the nonterritorial part of any airport.

and snowboard cases on top; (3) small roller bags always in the front-most portion, nearest to the cargo door; and (4) don't plan at all: throw it all in and try for a grand, chaotic pyramid that somehow stays intact. The fourth technique seemed to be the most common. I learned to always leave room for the inevitable five to twenty carry-on bags that were too big for the mini overhead bins or for under the seats of the CRJ, and therefore had to be crammed in at the last minute, which was like the bonus round of this game of Tetris.

Instead of losing the game when I could not fit a piece in place, usually I just ended up with a badly bruised shin, pinched fingers, crushed toes, or a hard-sided golf case careening into my head as I waited for the next bag to make its way up the belt-loader conveyor.

On any given day, I would go through this routine several times throughout my shift. After a while, loading baggage didn't feel like a game anymore. It felt like work.

No Longer New

New airplanes smell like the future. The CRJs that flew in and out of Bozeman were brand new, and they gave off fresh scents of molded plastic, machined metal, and supple leather. Even the grease around the landing gear had an aromatic quality and an

The object produced by airports, the traveler, now stands opposed to the airport as an alien being.

appealing opacity. The lettering on the side of the planes was bold and unmarred, and the aircraft doors opened with a satisfying *click suck pop*.

But I recall one day when the aircraft landed in Bozeman and the wings of the plane were covered with dents and nicks in the paintjob. There had been a major hailstorm in Denver, and the CRJ no longer had its fresh-from-the-factory sheen. In my job training, we had learned about how critical it was that the flying surfaces of the aircraft were never, ever compromised—but this plane was clearly going to take off again in twenty-five minutes and make its way back to Denver.

During my first few weeks at the airport, it seemed crucial to distinguish a serious risk from standard operating procedure. Once the job was no longer new, though, flight ceased to seem so delicate. Eventually, many of the nose cones of the CRJ aircraft were off color or outright bare, suggesting quick replacements at some hub, no time to worry about consistent paintjobs. Day in and day out, planes landed and planes took off, and over time everything at the airport became grimy. Gradually, I realized that the futurity promised by the airport had been tarnished. An analogy might be drawn that flight is really all about the past. Airplanes are no longer new, and we expect less and less from them.

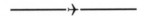

To valorize airports through an affirmation of a return to the soil is to place passengers in an impossible bind.

Tom

My favorite coworker at the airport was Tom. Tom was a big Montana cowboy who managed to at once fulfill and defy every stereotype inherent in that initial description.

Tom was the hardest worker at the airport: he could handle baggage more efficiently and systematically than anyone else I knew. But he was also playful: he treated the tarmac like a rodeo ring, driving the TUGs around like they were his mechanical bucking broncos. Tom also loved to sashay across the tarmac twirling the heavy black rubber chocks that went around the aircraft landing gear.

Tom was a strapping hulk of a guy, and he could be very intimidating to rude passengers: he wouldn't take any guff from passengers jockeying rudely for First Class upgrades, nor would he mince words over a lost bag. Tom was all business.

Tom had been in the Navy and had three daughters from a previous marriage. He drove a Ford F-350 SuperCab, and when we'd finish our shifts, Tom would peel out of the employee parking lot smirking at me in his rearview mirror, back tires spitting gravel. Tom could be a show-off, but he was also a good listener. Sometimes when the inbound flight was delayed, we would sit for hours telling each other the stories of our lives, and

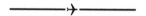

The airport is a vestibule in which a spiritual sense of things disappears, and material sense unfolds the gritty facts of existence.

Tom would always listen intently to my postcollege existential musings and life questions.

One time as we were heading out to meet the noon arrival, Tom noticed that I was wearing my SkyWest baseball cap backward. Tom gave me a lascivious sideways look and drawled, "There are only two times when I wear a hat like that: when I'm riding my bike, or when I'm sucking someone off." That was classic Tom, getting in a little moment of gay fun before hard work, the long plane advancing toward us and the roar of the reverse thrust winding down.

Tom manned the jet bridge while I marshaled the aircraft into the gate; Tom gently nudged the beeping bridge up the plane's side, a snug fit. I moved the baggage cart into position and started unloading luggage, while Tom welcomed the deplaning passengers to Bozeman.

After all the passengers were off the plane and the luggage was hurled onto the moving belt of the baggage claim, Tom and I had to go up to the airport restaurant and get buckets of ice for the next flight. We had to unpack a box of SkyMall catalogs that had just been delivered to United. We had to load the outbound baggage, and finally we had to board the outbound passengers pronto. We only had about thirty minutes to make this all happen and have an on-time departure—our airport's reputation was counting on it. The corporate representative who

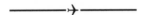

What is interesting about airports is not their dramatic content but their embryonic form.

had stopped by our airport the week before reminded us that we were an important team in the SkyWest family.

Tom was a real worker and a good friend, and working with him made those long days go by quickly. A few years after I left Bozeman, I got an e-mail from Tom inviting me to his wedding—he was marrying another cowboy, with whom he'd built a ranch somewhere in eastern Washington. I couldn't make it to the wedding for one reason or another, and I regret not going. He was a great friend.

Now whenever I see someone wearing a baseball cap backward, I think of Tom sucking someone off. I think of Tom, and I think of all those evenings after the last departure of the day, each of us in our matching navy blue outfits, little United logos flashing proudly as we raced our TUGs slowly back to the SkyWest garage, into jet exhaust sunsets.

FOD

FOD was one of the corporate acronyms I learned during my initial job training. It stands for Foreign Objects of Debris. Sometimes, if you look out of an airliner window, you may see a nondescript barrel on the tarmac with those letters faintly stenciled on it: FOD. This always reminded me of the trashcans

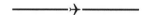

The airport is resolutely committed to partiality, irony, intimacy, and perversity. It is oppositional, utopian, and completely without innocence.

at McDonalds or Burger King that say THANK YOU on their flaps.

Whenever there was slack time between flights, we cross-utilized agents were instructed to rove around the tarmac searching for FOD. FOD could include Ziploc baggies (usually just the zip parts would be left), soda can lid tabs, errant screws, bent washers, or rusted nuts. But most commonly, FOD consisted of small plastic wheels and metallic hubs broken off cheap roller bags heaved in and out of the cargo holds. While picking up this certain species of FOD, I often thought of that flashy commercial for a fancy roller bag, how the classy traveler whizzes through the airport to catch his flight, pulling his slick race car roller bag—and then the ad cuts to another poor schlub with an overstuffed duffel bag who bumps into other travelers, trips over things, and eventually hobbles up to a gate that says FLIGHT DEPARTED.

Another regularly found type of FOD are zipper pulls—but never ones that read YKK. If you were to get down on your hands and knees on any tarmac and start crawling around, you would find a zipper pull within a few minutes. The narrow end would be severed or shattered where a baggage handler scraped the side of the bag it belonged to against a stronger metal edge. There are probably millions of derelict zipper pulls scattered around airports all over the world, accumulating slowly like an

The easiest thing of all is to pass judgments on airports; it is more difficult to grasp them, and most of all difficult to do both together.

abandoned currency, waiting to be excavated by archaeologists of the future.

Trouble

Sometimes at the airport I got in trouble. Once I got the job, I let my hair grow back out, and one day Lance called me into his office when we had a lull between flights. He told me to have a seat, and I sat across from him at his managerial desk. The corkboard next to his desk displayed various awards that our airport had recently won: "95% On-Time!" "Excellence in Customer Support." "Manager of the Month."

While I sat there shifting around in the plastic chair, Lance flipped through a large three-ring binder, tracking the section headings with his finger. He found what he was looking for, and rotated the binder around for me to see, sliding it forward and keeping his index finger steady on a certain paragraph:

Employee Hair Length for Males: Should not descend past ¼ inch of shirt collar.

I was in trouble. But no words were directly spoken about this infraction. It was understood that I was in violation of corporate policy, and that I would get a trim. (I don't remember actually

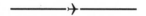

A rumble comes from the airport's deep core. It is more than the mutter of powerful underground baggage systems.

getting a haircut that time; I must have done it myself, or maybe it got super cold and I wore a winter cap for a while during this time.)

Then there were the black shoes. We were supposed to wear plain black shoes while on duty. Mine were dark gray, a particular style that I liked, and they were comfortable for both extremes of the job: long periods of standing and hauling awkward baggage around. Lance never said anything, but would often look down at my shoes with a slightly furrowed brow, a barely discernible slight head shake.

During the summers I had another part-time job, guiding daily kayaking tours in Yellowstone National Park. I would camp in the park and lead trips for a couple of days between my airport shifts, then speed the 90 miles or so out of the west entrance to the park and up the Gallatin Canyon back to Bozeman. I recall stints of this back and forth that lasted weeks on end with no days off, and my United uniform during those busy weeks was well worn to say the least. From the outside, I was not the model SkyWest employee, in my rumpled uniform; but I was reliable on the tarmac and even earned a few customer service posters of recognition myself. (I had a way with delayed passengers.)

I never got in trouble formally for my less than pristine appearance, but I did worry about it whenever I saw my navy blue pants, dark gray shoes, and rumpled United shirt bunched scrunched up in my backseat alongside my kayaking life jacket

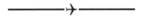

The airport contracts about you. It is a sharp-edged, massed, metallic airport.

and raingear, as I pulled away from shore of Yellowstone Lake, still wearing my river shorts and sandals, bound for the airport but halfway between two very different professions, two very different landscapes, both infused with the aura and expectations of the West.

Creatures

At first I only saw airplanes and people: flying machines, and the human passengers that would go in and out of these machines. The longer I worked in this odd environment, however, I started to notice something curious: there were creatures at the airport everywhere I looked.

First there were the inanimate ones: a stylized V of Canada geese sculptures hanging from the terminal ceiling; the big bronze grizzly bear sitting at the base of the escalators; even a sculptural cougar, frozen in flight, leaping out over the baggage claim. These pieces of art were supposed to evoke the Wild West, an idea of animals running free across the frontier . . . right through the modern airport.

Gradually I began to see more lively creatures abounding at the airport—lively even when sometimes dead. For instance, one June afternoon the United Express CRJ descended smoothly, landed gracefully, and taxied to the gate like any other day.

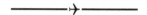

Passengers wait out delays like caged animals, sweating and stupid. One should remember that there are interesting views on the ground, too.

My coworker Misty marshaled the aircraft in, and when the plane jerked to a stop, I crawled under the wing to place the chocks around the landing gear—standard operating procedure. As I scooted under the wing and swung the heavy rubber triangular blocks around the aft wheels of the plane, the smell was familiar yet also peculiar: the usual aroma of aviation fuel exhaust, but mixed with . . . something else. I suddenly became aware of red splotches dotting the belly of the plane: blood. Then I noticed a quarter-size piece of bone or brain that had been thrown up into the landing gear cavity.

As I squirmed out from under the plane, the captain clambered down the steps and jogged over. He shouted over the Auxiliary Power Unit (APU) screaming in the background, "A jackrabbit hopped out onto the runway just as we landed! We clipped him good! Woo wee! Look at all that blood!" There were little chunks of flesh and fur dangling from the wing flaps.

Meanwhile, the passengers deplaned, utterly oblivious to the minor scene of horror behind them. My coworker and I unloaded the baggage, boarded the outbound passengers, and turned the plane around in the obligatory thirty minutes. The pulverized remains of the jackrabbit flew to Denver, and onward. This gave new meaning to the term "sky burial," which before this I had understood only in a Tibetan Buddhist context.

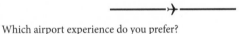

Which airport experience do you prefer?

Then there was the morning of the great Delta gopher snake. The 737 had overnighted on the tarmac one fall evening, and the next morning a huge gopher snake was discovered curled around the nose landing gear. Apparently the snake had crawled up into the landing gear cavity in Salt Lake City (or somewhere earlier), and then slithered down onto asphalt in Bozeman.

It occurred to me that this sort of counted as an evolved form of migration: the snake had found a rather quick way to a new bioregion. And then it dawned on me that, strictly speaking, evolution encompasses everything that happens; there's no getting outside of it. Airports are a human phenotype, and other creatures interpenetrate these techno-cultural spaces, showing them to be actual ecosystems, through and through. And years later, when I saw a poster for the movie *Snakes on a Plane*, I didn't think it sounded creepy or tantalizing—it seemed entirely plausible.

One time I walked out of the back room of the United baggage bay and noticed a mound of what looked like excrement clinging to the wall. On closer inspection, it was a bat that had hunkered down to wait out the day on the cool, shaded north face of the terminal. When I got closer, I saw how beautiful it was: slightly furry, more blue-gray than black, its tiny eyes watching me watch it.

But I could not tarry in this naturalist state of observation; there was a pile of luggage to load onto the plane. After loading

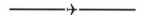

———✈———

In any discussion of the airport one must make it clear whether one is talking about the airport as a form of amusement or as a form of art.

the baggage, as I drove the TUG back across the tarmac, I watched from afar as one of my coworkers saw the bat and promptly crushed it with the end of a hard-sided golf club case.

I think antagonism toward other flying creatures is often heightened around airports, and not just because of the threat of airborne collisions. Other flying creatures also pique repressed fears that humans have overextended their reach in the world—a nagging worry that perhaps we shouldn't be flying at all. But again: if this is our phenotype, there will be no easy way to undo it.

Late one night I was in the middle of cleaning the inside of the aircraft, near the end of my shift. I was wiping a child's magic marker scribbles off the retractable window shade when I noticed a translucent, still insect lying between the plastic interior screen and the external pressurized glass pane. It was suspended in this space, its miniature wings extended so that I could see the points of articulation and its delicate yet refined flying surfaces. I was reminded of Virginia Woolf's essay "The Death of a Moth," which focuses intensely on a dying moth and concludes that death is stronger than us all. As I looked at the small bug, I wondered at what point had it become incarcerated between the plane's windowpanes. Did the moth get in the window recess in the factory, during the plane's construction? Or had this bug, in Santa Barbara or Denver, exploited a weak seam or gap in the

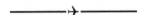

Precisely because they are a known model, airports impose certain standards from which too-marked deviations become impermissible.

plane's allegedly airtight construction? For how long had this plane always been a mobile sarcophagus of sorts?

Sometimes as planes would taxi to the gates, the pilots would radio in and request a "bug wipe." This meant that on descent they'd collided with a cloud of insects, and the smeared corpses would be coating the aircraft's cockpit windows, a hoary tapenade. There was a special ladder that I would carefully wheel up to the nose of the plane, and I'd climb up the ladder carrying a window wiper that was like those found at gas stations between pumps. I'd spray some generic cleaning fluid on the angled windows, and swipe and rub, swipe and rub, until all the bugs were gone, their minuscule bodies floating in a bucket of grayish blue, destined for the industrial drain on the tarmac. Bird strikes are a popular subject, raising questions of everyday danger and ecological significance. Bug strikes, however, are all but ignored, at once too small, vastly outnumbering, and myriad for most people to care about. But how many things do humans tune out, simply as a matter of scale?

Airport creatures tuned me in to some environmental aspects of human flight, to a sort of zoomed-out view of how we travel and how we come into contact with other beings across scales of time and significance. These experiences have caused me to wonder how air travel distances us from the reality of living with others, even as it also brings us closer together.

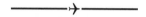

Airports are apparently obsessed with words.

Burnout

I understand why some people are terrified of flying. It's true that any ordinary flight might turn into a spectacular disaster.

One time during a lazy evening shift, I heard some commotion next door at the Delta counter. I peeked around the wall and saw the Delta crew huddled around their station manager. The Delta manager was talking in a hushed but urgent tone about their inbound flight. I pretended to be picking up rubbish off the terminal carpet, and listened.

Apparently one of the plane's engines had a burnout mid-flight, and it might turn into an emergency landing if the other engine went. The plane was twenty-five miles out. The airport fire trucks had been called and were rushing to the end of the runway, anti-fire foam at the ready. The faces of the Delta workers reflected a mixture of excitement, panic, and sudden bewilderment: cross-utilized agents were not trained to handle runway skids.

I raced around the check-in counter and through the supply room, out the United door, and watched as the Delta Connection CRJ descended between the Bridger peaks and the north end of the Gallatin Range. The landing lights winked on. The plane glided in elegantly and landed like all the others I had seen before, except for the three chartreuse fire trucks, lights flashing,

At the airport we are deposited in a unique, procedurally generated world.

that raced behind the plane—I remember thinking that the fire trucks' engines were louder than the plane's reverse thrust.

I was oddly disappointed. No crash landing, no harrowing escape by passengers jumping onto emergency chutes, no one calling on me to lend a hand, United and Delta workers joined in camaraderie. It was just another plane to be unloaded, cleaned, inspected, repaired . . . and sent off again into the blue.

I think I remember that the tail of the plane was scorched behind the engine that had burned out in flight. But I might have exaggerated or even invented the vision in my mind, mixed as it is with various movie scenes, headlines, and news photos of planes sitting at the end of the runway or off in a ditch, after an emergency landing or a botched takeoff.

Flight Privileges

As an airline employee I could fly for free, practically anywhere. Of course, flying for free not only meant flying standby: it also meant flying standby with lowest possible priority, below paying passengers trying to get on earlier flights, below pilots and other crew members, and below all the mainline airline employees. This made travel hard to plan, but this also made it exciting. I used my flight privileges as often as I could. I flew around the country to see friends and family, and sometimes just to Denver and back

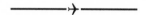

One can describe an airport by recording a sequence of actions, words, or gestures, but one cannot perceive an airport in its totality.

on a whim. There was something alluring about striking out for the airport and *not* knowing if I would be able to fly or not.

At the Gallatin Field Airport (as it was then called), we enjoyed what was called a "station agreement" between the airlines: any airline employee could fly standby (or "nonrevenue" in the parlance) on any of the other airlines. So, as a SkyWest United Express worker, I could fly standby not only on United flights, but also on Delta, Northwest, and Horizon (the regional carrier for Alaska Airlines). These flight privileges were a major perk for an airline employee. And yet, most of the people I worked with at the airport rarely used their flight privileges: they had families, second jobs, or worked full-time and therefore could not get away so easily.

You needed to be very flexible and spontaneous to fly standby as an airline employee: you'd take off for Denver, Salt Lake City, Minneapolis, or Seattle, and unless that was your endpoint, you'd likely have to make any number of uncertain connections in order to make it to your "final destination"—you might end up flying four different airlines, zigzagging all across the country, just to make it to San Francisco and back over a two-day break. Usually you'd return exhausted, and just in time for work. But if you had an adventurous spirit, it was a blast—it could be as wild as running rapids on the Snake River. Flying standby regularly also made the work more exciting, because a sense of

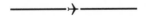

The critic's role is not to dissect airports for achieved transport but on the contrary to determine in them the vocation of their failure.

personal suspense started to pulsate through the entire network of flight: the whole operation seemed held together by thin threads of time and tenuously maintained spaces.

And yet the reality was that for most people who worked at the airport, it was just that: *work*. It was not an easy thing to fly for free, due to complex and constant scheduling, and neither was it a particularly unique or interesting job. In those days, the starting pay was around seven dollars an hour, and the hours were often miserable. The work was tedious, repetitive, and physically taxing: hefting several tons of awkward-sized luggage every day; standing in front of a computer screen checking in passengers and occasionally being castigated for incompetence over a weather delay somewhere across the country; transporting crates of soda cans out to the planes . . . these things quickly chipped away at the romance of flight. Furthermore, the chances for promotion were rather slim. I did see my operations manager, Lance, become the regional manager in Denver; and the supervisor Brad moved up to the new operations manager in Bozeman and then eventually went on to become the operations manager in Salt Lake City. So there was a kind of professional mobility, but rather than simply upward, it was more outward, angular, and dispersed.

If I Google my old coworkers today, I can find traces of their lives, like little lines of flight: snapshots of happy families in the

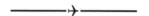

The airport is that which hands over every rendezvous to chance.

snow, or stylized Facebook profile pictures with familiar grins or serious looks, their hands holding beers or kids, sometimes making unclear gestures, maybe faux gang signs. For a time we all worked together at a small airport in Montana. The airline we worked for told us we were a "team"—but I wasn't sure who we were competing against, or when the game was supposed to end. On the other hand, what we were doing *did* have high risks, whether that meant breaking the aircraft, or finding oneself stranded in a remote airport amid a standby spree around the country, while trying to get back to work.

Stranded

One early spring day I used my flight privileges to hop over to Michigan to visit my parents. Because the flights were relatively empty, I flew First Class on Northwest both legs, Bozeman to Minneapolis, Minneapolis to Traverse City. It was the perfect standby excursion. I enjoyed an omelet on the first flight, and a second glass of Syrah as the next flight cruised past the Wisconsin shoreline and I looked down at the Manitou Islands in Lake Michigan.

A couple of days later, I had to fly back to Bozeman to work the next morning. I left plenty early, to give myself a full twenty-four hours to get home. The first flight went smoothly, Traverse City

Not ignoring what is good in airports, we should be quick to perceive airport horrors.

to Detroit, a fifty-minute hop across a state of decay. But I was excited to see the new Detroit airport, with its red bullet tram that whooshed above the concourse, connecting the farthest gates in a matter of minutes.

In Detroit I was waiting to catch a connecting flight to Salt Lake City when a classic Midwestern storm grayed out the sky, dumped heavy wet snow, and abruptly shut down the airport. I didn't have a cell phone at that time in my life, nor did I have a credit card to my name, and I had only about 15 dollars in my wallet.

So that night I slept on the floor of the brand-new McNamara World Gateway concourse. I was no longer a giddy First Class flier, but rather was relegated to the wretched status of a postmodern nomad. As I rolled out my highly compressible sleeping bag on the floor, I experienced the weird thrill of urban wilderness. The carpet, however, still smelled new, and had a certain firm softness to it. The fluorescent lights glowed through my closed eyelids, making for phantasmagoric dreams. Lulled by distant announcements for people to pick up the white courtesy phone, I fell into a deep sleep.

I opened my eyes at some point in the nether hours long past midnight, awakened by a strange sensation of synchronized motion and sound. I raised my head slightly and looked around, while trying not to draw attention to my humble bivouac.

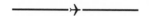

Circumstances supply only partial answers in airports.

About 50 feet down the concourse was a cleaning crew, working in total unison, their outfits as crisp and conforming as the new airport concourse that they were cleaning. Their vacuums and litter-plucking devices looked futuristic, and they roved expertly in and out of the departure gates, cleaning every seat surface, picking up every discarded boarding pass and Starbucks cup, and dropping them into sleek rolling and pivoting trashcans. They cleaned right around my sleeping bag, treating my prone body as another feature of the concourse—or more likely, having been trained not to disturb the passengers.

Little did they know that I was an ordinary worker, too, waiting out the night, hoping to catch a morning flight in order to get back in time for my shift. As I drifted back to sleep, I tabulated my chances of making it back to Bozeman on time, mentally mapping the routes my flight privileges could take to deposit me back at my airport, back to work.

Strange Flights

I had moved to Bozeman for a Master's program in English. My airport job paid the rent all spring and summer, as I covered many of my coworkers' shifts; within a few months I could practically run the airport by myself. I remember the startled look on passengers' faces when they'd see me boarding them at

In airports, when we are invited to rise above ourselves, so as to see the worst, as though to see the best, almost always we faint away.

the upstairs departure gate after having just checked them in for their flight downstairs a half hour ago; and then they'd see me outside a few minutes later loading their baggage onto the plane, before finally hopping onto the diesel pushback TUG and sending them down the taxiway.

Starting in the fall of 2001, my other part-time job commenced: teaching freshman composition three mornings a week as part of my graduate work. This involved reading the essays of dutiful ranchers' children and transplant trustafarians alike, with the former group having a more intuitive knack for descriptive prose.

September 11 was my day off. On my days off, when I was fly-fishing or hiking, I would find myself subconsciously tracking inbound flights and takeoffs, distant jet blasts and glints of silver in the sun. I remember the absence of planes that day as a kind of kink in the muscle memory that any job creates over time: where Delta's 737 usually flew overhead from Salt Lake City at noon, there was only silence and sky.

I was scheduled to work at the airport the following afternoon, on September 12. But first I had a class to teach. It was my first time teaching at the college level, and we were only a few weeks into the semester; I was twenty-three years old. I recall sitting in a discussion circle with thirty freshmen on that day, not really knowing what to say.

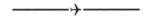

Airports can absorb and make shine through the concourses whatever people may want to save from the natural ruin of time.

As I tried to direct attention to our course anthology, I remember one student who was so upset that he blurted out in class, "We need to bomb people, NOW!"

When I tried, in my most affected professorial tone, to gingerly ask the class to consider the construction of the "we" in this claim, and whom exactly it was "we" should bomb, the same student screamed back at me, "*ANYBODY!*" His idea seemed to be that by inflicting firepower by air on other people, the United States could steal the show: the products of our military jets would be the focus of attention, and take away from the spectacle of four commercial airliners having gone rogue.

And a spectacle it was. When I walked over to the student union after class for lunch, I saw that several large TV screens had been wheeled into the open spaces between the seating areas. Some students filtered in and out of the dining hall like normal, scooping out helpings of macaroni and cheese; other students stood transfixed, watching reruns of the planes crashing again and again and again into the towers of the World Trade Center. The event was being familiarly looped, and the ambience of the instant replay created a warm, somewhat stale sensation—despite the chillingly fresh content.

That afternoon, I drove out to the airport for my shift. I had tried to call in to figure out if flights were on time, or if I even had to work—but the lines were all busy. I decided to play it safe

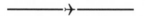

Time, unfortunately, though it makes animals and vegetables bloom and fade with amazing punctuality, has no such simple effect upon airports.

and just show up. When I got to the airport, the scene was one of stunted pandemonium. The terminal seemed at once totally chaotic and oddly frozen. Yes, my manager explained, I was still needed for work; but there were no flights due in or out that day. However, they could start back up at any moment—so we had to be ready.

In the meantime, there was a line of skittish passengers to deal with, people who were scheduled on flights that were not going to depart. These passengers didn't realize, perhaps, the scope of what had occurred the day before, how all the commercial airlines had simply been grounded into the unforeseeable future. Not that we airline employees knew any better: the best we could do was reschedule the passengers on flights a day or a week later, send them off with newly printed itineraries, and cross our fingers.

After assisting a dozen or so confused and distraught passengers who were feeling the logistical back-blow of what would come to be called 9/11, I went back into the break room and saw my manager Lance taping onto the wall a few photographs of himself directing a C-130 Air Force cargo plane onto our taxiway. This was one of the strange flights that had landed at our airport the day before; Lance had taken the roll of film to a one-hour photo lab that evening and had them printed out, and now was displaying them like little trophies. Lance told me excitedly

Airports, moreover, work with equal strangeness upon time.

that a stealth bomber had landed in Bozeman, too; but it had refueled and taken off again before anyone could get a picture of it.

The next day, I rummaged through the files on my desk, and found an essay that appeared in the Spring 2001 patagonia outdoor clothing catalog. This short piece was called "Homage to Faizabad," and it was written by the journalist Rob Schultheis; he was covering a drawn-out war in Afghanistan. The essay begins beautifully:

> We've been flying for nearly an hour, with nothing below us but the raw gorges and snow-covered peaks of the Hindu Kush. Somewhere down there are villages, fields, roads and trails, and the war we have returned to cover, but it's all lost in distance, space and scale in the vastness that is Afghanistan.

Schultheis goes on to describe the isolated town of Faizabad, including the friendly people he meets amid the wheat fields, pastures, and poppy fields. I took this essay to campus the following day and photocopied it for my students; in class, we took turns reading it aloud, slowly, paragraph by paragraph. We talked about the expository strategies that the author employed, including the initial focalizing mechanism of an aerial view; we also talked about the real people depicted in the

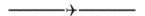

———✈———

An hour, once it lodges in the queer element of the airport, may be stretched to fifty or a hundred times its clock length; on the other hand, an hour may be accurately represented on the timepiece of the airport by one second.

essay, people caught up in a long history of conflicts and power struggles in this place freshly glossed in the news, Afghanistan.

Over the next several days, I kept arriving at the airport to work only to face passengers who felt immobilized, and who were becoming increasingly frustrated that air travel had not started up again. As airline employees, we were not trained to explain the conditions and contingencies of a national state of emergency—instead, we would concentrate in front of our computer monitors, fingers clicking away, and rebook the passengers on theoretical future flights, exuding less confidence by the day in the following day's departures. Still, it was our job, and so we carefully rescheduled passengers using a booking system that increasingly felt like dabbling in postmodern fiction: we were creating complex itineraries that would never be.

Some passengers came back to the airport day after day trying to fly out of Bozeman. Their travel clothes became rumpled looking, and they had less confidence on their faces every time they came through the sliding doors of the terminal. It became more of a travesty with each day: people showing up with full suitcases and long faces, only to trudge back to the long-term parking lot a couple of minutes later, after we had turned them away. Yet sure enough, one day a full plane flew in from Denver, and air travel was back on.

The thought of airports gets one through many a sleepless night.

By the end of the semester, I was teaching my students about narrative perspective, and we were discussing how things could be examined from multiple angles. My students read Mark Twain's "Two Views of the Mississippi," and we parsed his two takes on the riparian landscape: that of the Romantic river gazer, and that of the jaded riverboat worker. Now, it seemed as though there was a third perspective we needed to talk about, one that we had encountered in Schultheis's essay: the view from above. For at this point the news was flooded with aerial reconnaissance images of Afghanistan, including the Tora Bora region that looked not so unlike our own Tobacco Root Mountains stretched out across on the western horizon. There were contrails over those peaks; and on the news we could see weirdly congruous imagery of peaks on the other side of the planet, rendered by other planes with different intentions.

Like Twain's philosophical quandary about getting to know the river, and thus losing a sense of its innate beauty, our own romance with flight had become complicated. For myself, I could no longer treat the Bozeman airport as a simple workspace; I saw it enmeshed in politics and power, territory and populations. This was no mere "regional" airport—it was part of a fraught global matrix where all flights were strange flights, and travel was never an isolated endeavor.

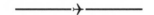

Airport madness is oftentimes a cunning and most feline thing.

Code Red

I worked with a woman named Vicki. At first Vicki was suspicious of me because I was a part-timer and a "college guy." But as I picked up more and more shifts for other workers, and proved myself to be a hard worker and a fast learner, she began to soften.

After about six months of Vicki scowling at me throughout our shifts together, one morning she signaled for me to follow her back into the garage where all the baggage carts were parked between flights. I didn't know what we were going to do back there, but I followed her anyway. Next to the baggage carts was our station refrigerator, where we stored all the extra sodas and bottled waters for the aircraft. Without a word, Vicki opened the freezer and pointed inside. Nestled in a small heap of ice were two half-frozen "Big Gulps" of Mountain Dew Code Red: one for her and one for me. The frosty treat was delicious, and the high-octane caffeine made the next work activities race by.

After that day, whenever we worked together, Vicki would buy me a Code Red, and we would go through the same ritual of discovering it in the freezer and then being excited about the cold slushy soda. We would drink it, and then go out to load bags or check the oil level on the TUGs and other vehicles. "Code Red" coincidentally sounded like the terrorist threat level at that time.

The airport's quenchless feud with time always seems yours, when you are in it.

Vicki had an impressive mop of orange hair and two children of indeterminate age and equally voluminous bright hair. Sometimes at the end of our shift, the kids would be waiting out in the employee parking lot with her husband in a rusted-out tan Jeep, and when Vicki and I would walk out of the unmarked side door of the terminal, the kids would be leaning into the jetwash of the Northwest Airbus 320s that arrived around that time. The kids got as close as they could to the chain link fence, trying not to get knocked down, hair whirling around and flaring up like little forest fires. When I said one day that her kids were cute, she looked at me like I was insane and told me they were ornery; it sounded like "on-ree" and took me a moment to understand.

One morning Vicki and I were working the seven o'clock flight together. We had boarded the passengers and loaded the bags, and were all ready to push back the plane from the gate to taxi to the runway. Vicki was operating the jet bridge, and I was on the tarmac making sure everything was clear behind the aircraft—that is what "wing walkers" do, those often bored-looking workers who you see holding plastic orange wands erect, standing near the tips of the wings while the plane moves back from the gate.

As Vicki reversed the jet bridge, pulling away from the CRJ, something caught on the gate, and there was a sharp *pop*. A cotter pin had snapped: the retractable stairs on the plane's

The airport is the only place from which we might begin to unsettle the very distinction between inside and outside.

front door slammed down, suddenly limp. We all stared at the twenty-million-dollar plane sitting there in the rising sun.

The jet bridge had snagged a tiny piece of the aircraft door. There was no serious damage to the flying surfaces of the aircraft, but corporate protocol required that we deplane all fifty passengers and reschedule them on different flights. One minute the aircraft had been ready for takeoff; the next minute we had a line of people holding useless boarding passes, and a plane that was going nowhere. Vicki was taken by Lance, to the local hospital for a mandatory drug test, another official protocol following any "incident." Short-staffed, the rest of us unloaded the baggage compartment of the plane and rerouted all the passengers on flights later that day. The pilots eventually "dead headed" the empty plane to Salt Lake City for repairs. It was a long morning, but by evening everything was back on schedule.

I never saw Vicki again. I heard a rumor that the drug test had come back positive for cocaine—but I heard lots of rumors at the airport, particularly after 9/11. I also heard that Vicki went back to work at Wal-Mart, where she had worked before the airport job opened up.

Ralph Waldo Emerson once wrote an essay called "Circles" that begins: "The eye is the first circle; the horizon which it forms is the second; and throughout nature this primary figure is repeated without end." I'm not sure that Vicki's circular path

Airports constitute the pathology of exile in its pure form: impoverishment of the inner world through the withdrawal of closeness.

from Wal-Mart to the airport and back to Wal-Mart was quite what Emerson had in mind—then again, the term "holding pattern" hadn't been invented yet, either. Somehow, circling planes make the geometry of the "primary figure" seem a little less spiritual.

Later that year, Mountain Dew came out with an orange soda called "Live Wire," but I never tried it.

Stickers

Soon after 9/11, a case of stickers arrived at the airport: this was the latest in a series of attempts to outsmart the terrorists.

The red stickers read SECURE, and we were instructed to place a sticker over each door seam on the aircraft whenever the plane was left unattended—whether this was in the daytime during a crew change, or overnight when the airport was all but abandoned. The idea was that if the plane had been accessed while left unattended, we would know by the stickers: they had a one-time-use seal and thus could not be reattached.

Imagine this scenario. Each day, the plane might be left unattended two or three times. Each time, the red stickers had to be deployed and then torn off when the plane was attended again. Within weeks, the doorframes of the aircraft resembled weird palimpsests, tacky material outlining the word SECURE at

In an airport, you may feel that you are living in conditions where it is both difficult and therefore necessary to say things not allowed.

a hundred different angles. We all shared a tacit understanding that we would continue to use the stickers, even though there would have been no possible way to determine if a sticker had been removed—there were so many bits and pieces of SECURE stickers stuck to the doorframes, a desperate demand for security in childish form and scattered indecipherably all over the planes.

Then one day, word came that we no longer had to use the stickers. The remaining rolls of stickers sat in a box in the corner of our office, accumulating dust, secure at last.

Jeff Bridges

I remember the cottonwood leaves were turning yellow when I saw it: the name Jeff Bridges on the passenger list printed out in the morning prior to our flights. Jeff Bridges and his three daughters would be checking in for a flight to Santa Barbara. We speculated that they had been spending some time at their home outside of Livingston, and were headed back to California for some interesting reason. Maybe it was the end of summer, and the girls had to be back in school. Or maybe it was for a movie. Either way, we started to recite lines from *The Big Lebowski* in anticipation of Jeff Bridges' arrival.

Our station manager Lance was very excited that Jeff Bridges would be checking in for our flight, and so he had positioned

In airports, far more than in any other place, wild rumors abound wherever there is any adequate reality for them to cling to and linger on.

himself steadfastly at the United counter in order to assist the famous actor when he arrived at the airport.

As luck would have it, Lance had to step away to a phone call in his office from St. George (company headquarters) at the precise moment that the Bridges pulled up to the curb in an old, beat-up Suburban. It was either dark gray or dust-coated black. I stood there looking earnestly into my computer screen, pretending to be busy. I shuffled blank ticket stock and carefully arranged the pens and stapler in a slot above the computer terminal. Jeff Bridges stepped out of the driver's seat and unloaded a surprisingly small number of bags from the rear of the Suburban. His daughters got out of the truck and stood in the glaring sunlight. They left the truck sitting there at the curb and approached the terminal, Jeff Bridges carrying a banjo or something slung over his shoulder, in a case. Then they walked through the sliding doors.

When he walked up to the United counter, I told Jeff Bridges that I had admired his performance as "The Dude." He thanked me and said, "Yeah, that was a pretty good show."

After looking carefully at Jeff Bridges' ID to make sure he was himself, and the daughters' IDs, too, I printed their boarding passes. It seemed slightly ridiculous, but I asked for and inspected all their IDs, because that is what I was trained to do—I was keeping the country safe. Their seating assignments were all in

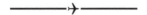

Completely dislocated—unable to be anywhere, really—in the airport, you take yourself far off from your own presence, and make yourself an object.

Economy Class; they were flying the entire way on our SkyWest CRJ aircraft, which at that point did not have First Class sections. I carefully explained their itinerary to them, making appropriate but not creepy eye contact, and I diagrammed how to get to the right gate in Denver in order to catch their connecting flight. Then I sent them on their way to the second level where the departure lounge was located. And this was curious: they left the Suburban sitting at the curb. I never found out what happened to it, whether it was supposed to be picked up by a friend, or whether it was towed and scrapped.

Jeff Bridges and his daughters waited for their flight to board like everyone else. Then the flight was delayed; and then it was canceled. It must have been a mechanical problem, because I remember rebooking a long line of passengers, sending them to Salt Lake City on Delta, or to Minneapolis on Northwest, or to Seattle on Horizon . . . instead of to Denver on United.

In the end, Lance got his chance to meet Jeff Bridges. When the passengers had all lined up back at the ticket counter again, Lance strolled out from his office and intercepted Jeff Bridges, who was waiting in line with everyone else; Lance ushered him and his daughters into the backroom, where the daughters lounged on our swivel chairs while Lance personally rebooked them on another flight. I was both impressed and a little put off: Why shelter these people and treat them like royalty, when they

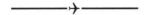

General feelings of dislocation in an airport aren't the problem. The problem is a localized feeling of dislocation concerning all airports.

were clearly comfortable standing in line with the rest of the disgruntled passengers?

Airports have a peculiarly strong way of reinforcing accepted social norms: it was as if my manager Lance had an obligation to shield the famous actor from the ordinary travelers. But this is me looking back at it now ten years on, reflecting on class systems, the society of the spectacle, and celebrity status. At that time, I was too busy rebooking other passengers to think about this kind of thing for very long. In any case, soon Jeff Bridges and his daughters were long gone, and we had another flight to deal with.

Night Shifts

When I started working at the airport, the job was exciting: crawling under airliners to place chocks around the landing gear was a real thrill. Gradually, the job became routine: it was work, and I found myself counting down the hours and then minutes until my shifts were over, punching a green paper card that recorded my units of labor.

The night shifts, however, were different. They were a relatively relaxed affair, and they had a kind of magic to them.

Here's what happened: the first hour involved waiting around the check-in counter and answering people's questions about if the flight was on-time—and if not, why not. Only two of us

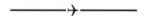

The airport's consciousness crudely swerves into its passions.

would be working on any given night, and once the flight radioed in that it was fifteen minutes from landing, we had to prepare the ramp for the arrival. Sometimes we would prepare things well ahead of time, so we could then wait until the last minute, racing out to greet the plane while it landed and started to taxi; other times, we would hustle out at the fifteen-minute mark and then rush around like maniacs getting everything ready for the aircraft. It depended on what TV movie was playing in our office, or how personal our confessions and commiserations had become in the quiet hours in the backroom.

When the plane touched down, we had to marshal it to the gate, deplane the passengers, unload the baggage from the aircraft, dump the baggage at the baggage carousel, rush back to the check-in counter to file missing baggage reports, and finally, after the passengers had gone and the day's paperwork was all complete, unclaimed luggage was corralled into an abject closet . . . then we had to clean the plane.

Usually one of us would return to the counter to take missing bag complaints and file the paperwork. The other one of us would head out to the plane and start cleaning. The first thing to do was to clean the inside of the lavatory. This involved spraying and scrubbing the surfaces of the sink and toilet seat, and replenishing the hand soap, paper towels, and toilet paper roll. Sometimes I would have to use the toilet myself before cleaning

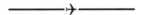

For reasons that are not well understood, airplanes are safer for most of us than airports.

it, and this always felt a little strange: sitting on the miniature plastic toilet in an otherwise empty, silent airplane parked for the night under dim lights. I was always nervous that my coworker would come bounding back onto the plane to help clean while I'd be sitting on the toilet—but it never happened. Still, I was paranoid, and so I would keep the flimsy door cracked, and watch through the oval window opposite the lavatory to make sure my coworker wasn't speeding across the tarmac in a TUG, back to the plane.

Once my coworker was back on the plane, we had to attend to the seatback pockets, clean the galley, and restock drinks, SkyMall catalogs, and emergency briefing cards. The last thing to do was to vacuum the plane. This is trickier than it sounds: our standard-size vacuum would be plugged into an extension cord from the jet bridge, and the cord had to be uncoiled, recoiled, and guided carefully as I moved through the plane; otherwise the cord could get hung up on the armrests, or get tangled around my ankles sending me sprawling into the aisle or across the seats. The easier job was using the handheld vacuum, going over all the seat surfaces—but for neurotic workers like myself, this could turn into a seriously tedious and time-consuming task, and Lance didn't like it if we went into overtime when it wasn't strictly necessary.

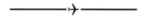

The airport is a lengthened tournament for flashing metal.

One time after my shift I slept overnight on the tarmac, in a baggage cart. That night my shift ended at around midnight and I had to be at the airport again in the morning at 6 o'clock. Why drive twenty minutes home for a miserable few hours of sleep? This seemed ludicrous. So instead, I had put my sleeping bag and my camping mattress in my work locker, and after feigning an exit to my coworker at the end of the night, I looped back inside the airport, went around the back of the check-in counter and out onto the tarmac. I walked stealthily toward our plane, and I crawled up into the second level of a nearby baggage cart.

In the upper compartment of the baggage cart, I laid out my camping mattress and unpacked my sleeping bag, spreading it out carefully. I took off my uniform and slipped inside the down baffles, shivering in the cold mountain air. I listened. It was quiet, the planes all tucked into their gates for the night. I pulled the vinyl curtain closed, and fell asleep.

This was perhaps some of the oddest "camping" I did during my time out west. I slumbered in a state of heightened awareness—but not for bears. My makeshift tent smelled slightly of well-worn luggage handgrips and avgas fumes. Still, it was camping under the Big Sky, and the mountains remained, indifferent forms on the horizon.

When I woke up it was just before dawn, and the Gallatin Range was beginning to turn pink. So was the plane next to me.

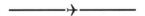

It is important to note that the effort to construct revolutionary airports has been part of the process showing the limits of being and time.

I rolled out of my sleeping bag, pulled on my rumpled United shirt and navy blue utility pants, hopped out of the baggage cart, and stuffed my gear into my backpack. Once I was walking across the tarmac, I was just another cross-utilized agent at work.

Ever since working at the airport, I always take care to clean up around me when I fly. I never put chewed gum in the seatback pockets, and I wipe up after myself when I use the lavatory. I make sure to give the flight attendants all of my refuse, and I don't spill snack-mix on my seat, where it might get wedged into little crevasses that someone will have to work extra hard to clean out at the end of the day. I also appreciate the views from the taxiway, even when they appear drab, the horizon smudges of gray. I remember that view from the tarmac at sunrise, when the runways were awash with bubblegum light, and the airplanes started to glow.

Cog

Thinking back on the various jobs I had held throughout high school, college, and after, working at the airport was by far the oddest—in part because it made real for me the expression of feeling like a "cog in the machine." Perhaps this was due to the fact that the job entailed working within concentric circles

Then a silence suffuses the airport, and a softness the traveler's eye; and the travelers no further question, and only the gate agents reply.

of machines, from the whirring ticket printers and baggage carousels, to the ground vehicles roving around the tarmac and the turbo-fanned airliners themselves thundering off into the blue, orange, or gray depending on the time of day. Work at the airport felt highly cyclical, as well, because the same patterns were repeated multiple times each day: enplane, deplane, unload baggage, load baggage, empty lavatory, fill lavatory. . . .

Of course this fact of sheer, relatively smooth repetition is in no way unique to airports; this is contemporary postindustrial life writ large. Nevertheless, there was something poignant about being in the midst of it while large turbofans screamed mad circles continuously throughout each day, powering down after landing or firing up in anticipation of takeoff.

Or maybe the cog-in-the-machine feel had to do with the fact that the work was so centrally scripted that we laborers could be rotated in and out of different airport locations. At the airline I worked for, there was a posted list of airports that needed temporary help, and you could put in a request for a short-term transfer to work at another airport for a week or two. The airline would put you up at a nearby hotel (at what I can only assume was a rock-bottom corporate rate), and then you could spend a weird sort of working vacation using your totally transferable skills to service other passengers and aircraft in a completely other geography. Everything was the same, yet different—noticeable

———✈———

For whom are we responsible at airports?

in unfamiliar coworkers' faces, and in the horizon line past the border of the airfield.

This was 2001, and I was still relatively fresh from the dramatic cinema experiences of *The Matrix* and *Fight Club*: these were two films that seemed to crystalize the traps and holdouts in the system of supermodernity—films that made you think about your place in the machine. They also both anticipated the mediascape of 9/11 and after. While *The Matrix* had pretty much nothing to do with airports (except, maybe, that scene where they go through the metal detectors to get into the skyscraper), *Fight Club* explicitly engages the culture of flight. Brad Pitt's Tyler Durden lampoons airline safety procedures, and Edward Norton's nameless narrator is an ordinary business traveler qua frequent flier whose life is being slowly whittled down by the drudgery of his trips; he too is a cog in the machine, and he fantasizes about its violent end.

My work experiences at the airport had a deep impact on me, tuning me into the system and its contradictions, and I continue to draw on my memories of this time as I research and write about air travel. Like my sensation of being a cog in the machine, I'm interested in the kinds of *feelings* that airports evoke or produce—for airport workers as well as for passengers inbound and outbound, passing through or interminably delayed. Airports can generate such strong feelings, as anyone who has

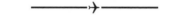

In airports, the zombie apocalypse has already occurred.

ever faced a sudden flight cancelation or unexpected upgrade to First Class can attest. On the other hand, even the most charged feelings produced by airports can dissipate at once, at the click of a button or at the thump of a suitcase on the carousel.

Working at the airport was a practice in mediation and modulation of these feelings, of life as a cog. Early on in the job I was excited about all the routine acts—like asking passengers if they'd had their luggage with them at all times. And I found the energy of travel contagious, as if I could draw from it simply by proximity. These feelings were rapidly muted as the work became monotonous and habitual, as any such work will tend to do to the worker after a while. Yet because of the nature of flight, there always seemed to be a peculiar need to perform a kind of uniqueness, as if to insist that travel was still novel, the pinnacle of progress—and not just another machine with well-worn cogs.

Six Years Later

After finishing my M.A. degree at Montana State University, Bozeman in 2003, I turned in my United uniform—that was the end of airports, for me.

I then moved to Davis, California, to start a Ph.D. program, where over the following six years I wrote a dissertation about

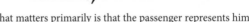

For the airport, what matters primarily is that the passenger represents himself to the gate agent, rather than representing someone else.

airports in American literature (much of this research would later be composted into my book *The Textual Life of Airports*).

In January 2009 I flew to New Orleans, where I was a finalist for a tenure-track position teaching contemporary literature and critical theory at Loyola University New Orleans. The poet Mark Yakich picked me up at the airport, and he took me to lunch at a Lebanese restaurant.

I had looked up Mark on the internet, but could find very little about him aside from a few intimidating interviews with literary journals (e.g., Interviewer: "What kind of car do you drive?" Mark: "Why does it matter? You think you'll be able to tell some deep personal quality about me from the make of my fucking car?").

In any case, I flew in nervous enough about the job, and even more nervous to meet this Yakich character. I could barely focus on the airports as I passed through them . . . my dissertation in full bloom all around me.

I hurried through the Louis Armstrong International Airport—an airport I'd never been to—and out to the curb, where Mark was waiting for me in a dark green Subaru Forester. (As if that matters.) By the time we were leaving the airport loop road, I had admitted to Mark that I once plagiarized a paper on *King Lear*, and Mark had admitted to me that he was terrified of flying. The trip was off to a great start.

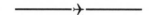

For what are the comprehensible terrors of shopping malls compared with the interlinked terrors and wonders of airports!

Over lunch we began talking about airport scenes in film and literature—a safe zone—and Mark mentioned how he'd recently finished writing a novel that had key scenes on a plane and in an airport. He then proceeded to rattle off some impressive factoids about historic plane crashes—he had the dramatic details memorized.

I had flown through Denver on my way there, where I saw the wreckage of Continental flight 1404, which just a few weeks before had skidded off the runway upon takeoff, bursting into flames and ending in a heap in a ditch alongside the runway, burning brightly in the night. Fortunately everyone on the plane survived, all the passengers escaping as the overhead bins melted over their heads. One passenger, upon exiting the plane, turned and snapped a picture of the plane with his camera phone, and posted it to Twitter. As my flight taxied to the gate in Denver, I saw the Boeing 737 cracked in half and sitting lopsided behind a hangar where it had been towed.

I described all of this to Mark, who looked up from his lamb kebob and appeared to be on the verge of crying or vomiting—I couldn't discern which—and then he began to tell me more about his fear of flying.

Through his stories of anxiety and imagination, Mark tuned me in to a whole other aesthetic register of flying, one that revolves around disasters of varying scales—all the incidents, accidents,

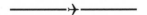

A successful airport emerges when disparate machines become a fluid dance.

and debacles that plague the history and the present of air travel. Mark also got me thinking back on, and writing more personally about, my experiences working at BZN; in all my literary analysis of airports, I had not tapped my own ethnography of airports. It was Mark who triggered the recollections that have appeared so far in this book, and it was Mark again who helped me with the aphorisms.

Airports are at once necessary and impossible.

Part Two

Travel

Droning

Some years later, I find myself amazed at the ways commercial air travel in the United States has changed—and at the ways it hasn't. The second part of this book muses on these changes and nonchanges, the new dilemmas and lingering problems of flight. Throughout the following pages, I pay special attention to the ways that airports *travel* throughout contemporary culture at large.

Consider this sentence from Don DeLillo's short story "Hammer and Sickle":

> It was a beautiful thing to see, aircraft climbing, wheels up, wings pivoting back, the light, the streaked sky, three or four of us, not a word spoken.

We might be tempted to read this description as a testament to the sublimity of human aviation. In fact, this scene is conjured from the perspective of maximum-security prisoners who are on work detail, cleaning up the tarmac of an Air Force base while jet fighters thunder indifferently around them. Like so many of DeLillo's descriptions of air travel, the ostensibly simple beauty of human flight just barely conceals a hideous underbelly.

Now we can imagine a similar scene wherein the aircraft themselves are "unmanned" or piloted by remote control. In other words, they might be drones. "Unmanned aerial vehicles"—UAVs,

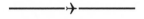

How do we conceive of the outside of an airport?

or drones—represent an increasingly contested nexus for public and secret discussions about airspace, privacy, police jurisdiction, and remote military targets. And they're bleeding into everyday life. In a roundabout way, drones too are a frayed end of airports.

In a 2012 *New Yorker* article on the private company AeroVironment, Nick Paumgarten surveys the many current experiments, speculative uses, and visionary futures of drones—from the deployment of a Predator drone to assist in a SWAT invasion of a ranch in North Dakota, to a "Tacocopter" that "theoretically delivers tacos to your door," to the small-scale "Hummingbird," crafted with enough verisimilitude so as to confuse actual Trochilidae. In the very same issue of the *New Yorker*, a "Talk of the Town" piece called "Occupied" centers on the duo who created the Occupy Wall Street drone, "a kind of four-pronged Frisbee that glides over Lower Manhattan, armed with a video camera, to keep tabs on the police."

Far from being solely the domain of covert government operatives and paramilitary independent contractors, we find ourselves in an era of ubiquitous droning. The US military was reported to have "some 7,000 aerial drones" as of mid-2011. But then, simply perform a search for "drone" on Amazon and behold the over 7,000 results, starting with a smattering of giddily advertised toy spy-devices; or consider the Sunday, May 27, 2012, cartoon strip in the *New York Times* by Brian McFadden,

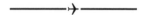

It is the grayness of the airport that above all things intrigues me.

entitled "The Many Uses of Police Drones." These comical (yet in several cases already existing) "many uses" include "Backyard Inspections, Traffic Enforcement, Pedestrian Enforcement, Fashion Policing, Disenfranchising Voters, Stifling Dissent, and Fourth Amendment Circumvention." Drones are everywhere—literally (at least potentially), as well as throughout our cultural imagination.

Indeed, at one point in his *New Yorker* article, Nick Paumgarten notes, "It will soon be technically feasible, if culturally unimaginable, to deploy passenger and cargo planes with empty cockpits." As much as we may be loath to imagine it, drones could transport *us* in the near future.

Yet a 2011 *Fast Company* article on concept aircraft designs, quite counter to its promising title—"NASA Reveals the Weird and Wonderful Commercial Airliners of 2025"—seems to reveal only that future jetliners will look basically like today's aircraft. And the possibility of remote piloting is not mentioned once in this article as an option or prospect.

The current state of air travel has two sides. On the one hand, aircraft are being miniaturized and controlled remotely, reducing human error in-flight and opening up innumerable possibilities for military operations as well as for ordinary people on the ground. On the other hand, flight seems determined to reproduce itself more or less as it is, promising evermore hours

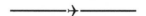

That airports have become the supplement of society is more than a catastrophe.

of tedium and waiting between (and inside) large rooms cruising through space.

These two sides twist and become one where new media technologies enter the scene. Whether manipulating a Parrot AR.Drone Quadricopter (marketed as "Controlled by iPod touch, iPhone, iPad, and Android Devices"), checking in for a routine flight on one's mobile phone, or dealing with labyrinthine realities of airport life (as one *New York Times* headline put it: "After the Plane Gets You to the Airport, an App Comes in Handy"), mobile communications devices are increasingly called on for navigation purposes—to supplement, as it were, the human body in flight.

During a radio interview about airports on the program "To The Best of Our Knowledge," I once quipped that Facebook could potentially outpace airports as the ultimate hubs for people's connections such that humans might stop flying altogether. Throughout my research and writing about airports, I have often wondered about the aura of exception that air travel evokes. I am continually puzzled by how, in an age of so many other technological advances over the past twenty years, airports have managed to retain their status as extraordinary places that demand a strange sort of seriousness and near piety. In a world where social networking can facilitate revolutions, and where connections happen as easily online as off, it seems inevitable

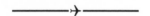

Remember, I am not recording the airport visions of an adman.

that moving hundreds of bodies around in large vessels will go out of fashion.

It isn't as though I truly believe that Facebook will become the twenty-first-century transit zone. It's more that distinct aspects of airports (including high demand for entertainment, feelings of "dead time," anxieties about contingencies) have anticipated and helped to pave the way for a host of newer experiences that are more about on-demand mediation and information (and capital) flows—and less about human bodies actually *going places*.

The human body is always in the picture, of course. There is always an experienced plain, a phenomenal range—whether it's a craggy mountain or a keyboard, a river eddy or an earbud. Human air travel will most likely be around for some time yet. But drones—particularly the nano-drones of the next generation—suggest that there is a critical convergence on the horizon, where remote sensing and screen culture might displace today's commonplace demand for airbuses.

Ubiquitous droning calls attention to myriad landscapes of flight. It is sitting in front of a computer monitoring remote locations. It is distinguishing between birds and bots. It is a chorizo taco on its way, tracked on a screen in your palm. It is a speeding ticket that records you going too fast when (you thought) no one else was around. And it is also the bulky plane we still line up to get on, if only as a negative assessment rubric. As Major

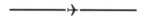

When airport restrooms double as tornado shelters, I feel some kind of sweet revenge on gender.

Michael L. Anderson, a doctoral student at the Wright-Patterson Air Force Base's advanced navigation technology center, noted about the next generation of drones: "It's impressive what they can do . . . compared to what our clumsy aircraft can do."

I do not know the future of drones. I'm not sure how they will transform commercial air travel, how they will affect that everyday experience that we can't yet quite imagine will be any different from how it currently exists. But I suspect that drones will continue to borrow from—perhaps eventually replace—the sensations and expectations that are uniquely found during air travel.

Another DeLillo passage, this one from his 1997 novel *Underworld*, is suggestive of this line of inquiry:

> There was a noise that started, a worldly hum—you began to hear it when you left your carpeted house and rode out to the airport. He wanted something friendly to read in the single sustained drone that marks every mile in a business traveler's day (252).

This passage is about a character's choice of airport reading, yet the "single sustained drone" is an uncanny instance of prescience. It portends the proliferation of these so-named devices that promise both constant war and its obverse side: the banality of military-grade existence.

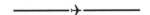

———✈———

The airport runs everywhere and is completely still at the center.

Plate 1 *SkyWest TUG at Bozeman airport © Christopher Schaberg.*

Plate 2 *Northwest DC-9 at Bozeman airport © Christopher Schaberg.*

Plate 3 *Eames tandem sling seats (Herman Miller, 1962) in Detroit Metropolitan Airport © Christopher Schaberg.*

Plate 4 *Futuristic airport seats in* 2001: A Space Odyssey *Dir. Stanley Kubrick © MGM, 1968.*

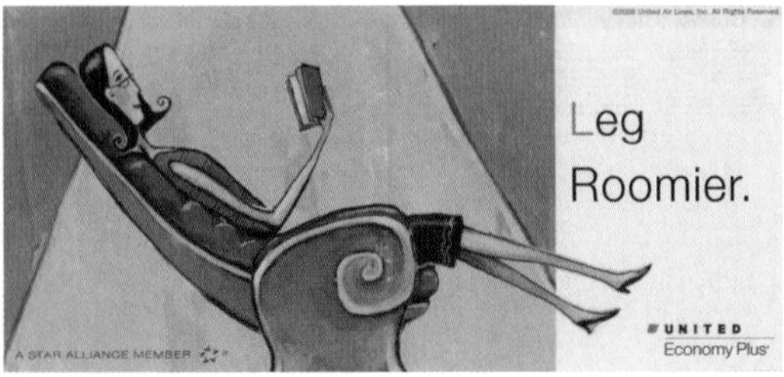

Plate 5 *Economy Plus advertisement on boarding pass sleeve © 2006 United Airlines.*

Plate 6 *BAE 146 at Chicago O'Hare airport © Christopher Schaberg.*

Plate 7 *Google Satellite View, Pinal Airpark, Arizona.*

Plate 8 *Southwest Boeing 737 at Sacramento airport © Christopher Schaberg.*

Plate 9 *The Southwest Experience, © 2013 Southwest Airlines Co. (used by permission).*

Plate 10 *Toothed exhaust duct covers on a Boeing 787, © Eric Prado, Wikimedia Commons.*

Plate 11 *Dreamliner preparing for departure at Houston airport © Christopher Schaberg.*

Plate 12 *Tarmac romance in* Casablanca *Dir. Michael Curtiz © Warner Bros., 1943 and in* Play It Again, Sam *Dir. Herbert Ross © Paramount, 1972.*

Plate 13 *The jet bridge in* Punch Drunk Love, *Dir. Paul Thomas Anderson © 2003 Columbia.*

Plate 14 *The jet bridge in* Killing Them Softly, *Dir. Andrew Dominik © 2012 Plan B.*

Plate 15 *A jet bridge at the Traverse City airport © Christopher Schaberg.*

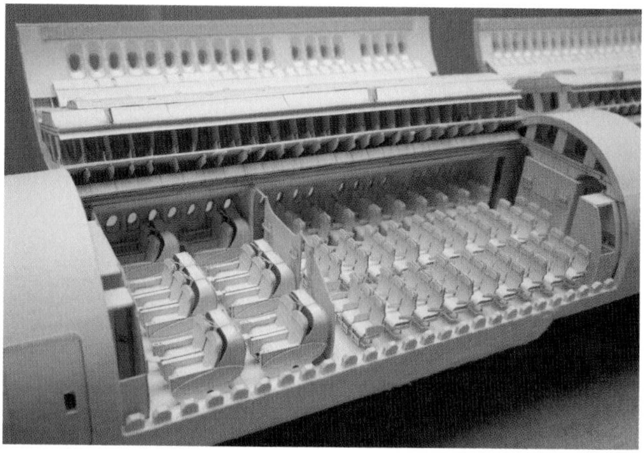

Plate 16 *Model 777 photo © Luca Iaconi-Stewart (used by permission).*

Plate 17 *Airport carpet in Bozeman © Christopher Schaberg.*

Plate 18 *Airport floor tiles in Houston © Christopher Schaberg.*

Plate 19 *Underground light tunnel in Detroit Metropolitan Airport © Christopher Schaberg.*

The historical, mutually constitutive conjunctions of military and civilian aviation have been well documented and accounted for. What we need next are subtle analyses of how the most quotidian new media practices and ordinary travel experiences are co-shaping one another, and perhaps mutating at scales that go far beyond the human in both directions.

Looking out of a window seat at 35,000 feet, zooming way out with Google Earth, seeing the world through the camera eye of a Hummingbird drone—these sorts of experiences de-center the human being, even as they imply human control. They communicate that humans are merely one species migrating around merely one planet in a vast universe. And they are also about the levels below: the informational, computational, entomological, bacteriological, elemental. These are other versions of the "worldly hum," to use DeLillo's phrase, that air travel brings into the foreground—a resonance made all the more acute by the presence of ubiquitous droning.

Seats

The elimination of speed

While writing this book I have traveled, usually sitting in cramped coach seats in commercial airliners. This is a commonplace

---

There is an extraordinary discrepancy between time on the clock and time in the airport.

comportment shared by many humans at the turn of the twenty-first century. The experience threatened to reach a level of absurdity in late 2010, when the *New York Times* travel journalist Joe Sharkey reported on a concept model stand-up aircraft seat called the SkyRider, which would radically reduce a passenger's personal space, and increase aircraft capacity and profit margins for airlines. The headline for Sharkey's column read "Legroom Tight Now? New Seat Is Less Spacious." Sharkey described the feeling of the seat as such: "like being strapped tightly into an amusement park thrill ride" (Sharkey, *The New York Times*).

This hyperbolic description of the SkyRider reveals an implicit understanding about commercial air travel: it is *not* supposed to feel like a wild ride. Ideally, air travel should be comfortable, uneventful, and entirely bland.

Sharkey's presupposition is a contemporary, low-grade variation on a theme articulated by Roland Barthes some fifty years before the emergence of the SkyRider. In his 1957 essay "The Jet-man," Barthes saw in the figure of the jet-pilot "a motionless crisis of bodily consciousness" (71) that results from being totally disconnected from the terrain: jets go so fast, and are so hermetically sealed, that pilots lose bodily awareness of the space over (and through) which they travel. Barthes explains this as a kind of diminishment of the older airplane pilot, who was perceived as a hero who hurtled through *felt* space.

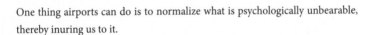

One thing airports can do is to normalize what is psychologically unbearable, thereby inuring us to it.

The crux for Barthes lies in a critical inconsistency that has to do with speed and bodily position:

> What strikes one first in the mythology of the *jet-man* is the elimination of speed: nothing in the legend alludes to this experience. We must here accept a paradox, which is in fact admitted by everyone with the greatest of ease, and even consumed as proof of modernity. This paradox is that an excess of speed turns into repose. (71)

The codes and protocols of the new era of jet-propelled flying machines caused "a sudden mutation" that forfeits the thrill of mobility in exchange for a feeling of motionlessness, and trades daring adventure for a kind of pseudo-religious devotion. According to Barthes, the old pilot-hero was defined by "speed as an experience, of space devoured" (72). The jet-man, however, goes faster than speed, all the way to stillness—or as Barthes puts it, the jet-pilot is assimilated into "pure passivity" (73). For Barthes this shift is apparent in a certain angle of repose adopted by the jet-pilot: experiencing the time of air travel comes to mean sitting absolutely still, in a rather relaxed position.

Over the latter half of the twentieth century and into the twenty-first century, Barthes's paradox seems to have made its way out of the cockpit and into traveling populations at large. The elimination of speed ironically increased with the spread of

In a world without heaven, airports are endings—more poignant than partings, profounder.

commercial aviation, and resulted in more collective time for airborne passengers sitting in rows of cramped seats, waiting to land. Commercial flight basically disseminates the peculiar feeling by which excessive speed turns into collective acts of passive repose.

Where Barthes was concerned with how jet thrust pushes humans bodies back in their seats and thus strips pilots of their humanity and heroic potential, Joe Sharkey basically accepts the object-ness of passengers as the default mode: people traveling in jets *should* be sitting back; they should not feel the speed with which they are hurtling through space (again, it shouldn't feel like an amusement park ride). What's at stake here appears to be a subtle downgrade in the assessment of human flight. Where Barthes's earlier observation noted a shift from human to inhuman, contemporary critiques of commercial flight take for granted the dehumanized standard of air travel.

But what if we accepted from the outset that human beings in flight are *objects* as much as they are *subjects*? In other words, what if we asked a different kind of question, aslant from Barthes's concern with how jet propulsion changes the human subjects of flight; what if we asked *how do these flying objects stay the same*? What kind of objects are people when they fly?

Interestingly, cultural representations of air travel have already provided speculative answers to this question, and they

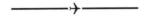

Far from equilibrium, the airport can become a bifurcation point or site of a swerve.

are organized around the figure of interest for both Joe Sharkey and Roland Barthes: how people in flight are *seated*. The present book finds these speculations to be strewn about the history of air travel. Over the following pages, I will show how various angles of seating throughout the hyperaesthetic culture of flight imagine humans as objects of air travel.

From space to time

Barthes identified the elimination of speed as a consequence of spatial surfeit: since the jet moves so fast across so much space, the bodily experience of that very same space is diminished, and the excessive speed turns into repose—being reclined in the aircraft seat. However, there is also a temporal factor at play. It is readily accepted that air travel *saves time*. Yet it is also widely admitted that the time of flight can feel excruciatingly drawn out, and experienced as profoundly *wasted* time: hours and minutes to be suffered and gotten *through*. In other words, air travel promises a way to skip over a longer temporal experience of a ground excursion or sea voyage; but flight then presents the passenger with highly concentrated forms of time to be mitigated, as when one waits in an airport departure lounge or while on a plane en route. Air travel reveals or unwraps the experience of *time* for flying objects—an experience to be expedited as much as possible, lest time feel to be at a standstill.

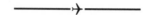

The reason why we should be cautious with airports is that hidden variables have become packaged in such a way as to resemble control.

It would seem that contemporary air travel reverses a popular slogan, insisting that it is not the journey but only the destination that matters. This is why Joe Sharkey doesn't want airplane seats to feel like a roller coaster ride: we're not in it for the adventure, but only to get from point A to point B as quickly and as painlessly as possible. Yet it's precisely this *painlessness* that bothered Barthes: perhaps such an endeavor—that is, flight—*should* be rather painful.

The treatment of space in either formulation—that certain geographies can (and should) be flown over and avoided—has obvious ecological implications: it is hard to conceive of the planet as interconnected and interdependent when certain specific places are privileged above vast tracts of other spaces. But the matter of temporality is no less ecologically vexed by air travel. When time is treated as savable, expendable, or disposable, the very present can begin to take on a strange quality: cushioned by the elimination of speed, travelers may feel disconnected from the time of travel, yet also all too intimate with the seconds and minutes elapsing therein.

Lingering—and not quite on purpose

There is a prehistory to trace here, akin to Barthes's elimination of speed but before the rise of jet propulsion. F. Scott Fitzgerald's unfinished novel *The Last Tycoon* (published posthumously in 1941) takes place in the late 1930s, and begins with the narrator

One of the limits of airports presents itself on the taxiway, when the planes, baked through long days, are piled in rows.

Cecelia on a coast-to-coast flight. At one point, Cecelia reflects on the experience of air travel with a telling observation: "We were all lingering—and not quite on purpose" (5). This scene unfolds with Cecelia acting blasé about the "fasten seatbelts" sign when the plane hits turbulence, and basically experiencing commercial flight as an utterly mundane event, and one that takes time in an annoying way. It would thus seem that the elimination of speed and its temporal discontents were already well established within a few decades of the birth of flight, even while still propeller-driven.

When Cecelia's flight is suddenly grounded due to violent thunderstorms, in the Nashville airport Cecelia meditates further on the ennui of flight—this time, on waiting to fly again: "We were taking off in less than an hour. Sleepy-eyed travelers appeared from the hotel, and I dozed for a few minutes on one of those Iron Maidens they use for couches" (14). This passage is of note because Barthes's elimination of speed seems to translate to an experience of being *on the ground*, as well.

Whether waiting to fly *or* soaring along at cruising altitude, Fitzgerald's characters express feelings of malaise: always "lingering—and not quite on purpose." These literary fragments suggest a subtle if also devastating critique of human flight: the feeling of flight is equated with the feeling of being on the ground. Air travel exposes *time-saving* and *wasted time* to be bound in

The airport nightmare is simple, because it is routine.

a tight knot, and the figure of this dilemma is materialized in humans as objects *sitting still.*

Cecelia refers to the furniture in the Nashville airport as "Iron Maidens"—or nineteenth-century torture devices, where humans are rendered as objects (in a bad sense) par excellence. And as noted just above, for Cecelia, sitting in the airport is rhetorically equated with the feeling of being on the airplane. By equating flying with sitting around at the airport, and sitting around the airport with an older form of torture, Cecelia has twice undermined the promises of air travel to save time and to propel one into the future. Rather, flight is seen as something that exposes people as objects of other devices.

It turns out that this equation of flying through the air and sitting on the ground has an interesting precursor, as well. In the 1920s airports often placed wicker rocking chairs in the waiting rooms; these rockers materially echoed the lightweight wicker seats used in early passenger planes. By this interior design strategy, the furniture in the airport got passengers ready for the thrill of flight by a metonymic segue: the airport could be phenomenologically linked to an airplane, just by sitting down.

If the wicker seats in the waiting room anticipated the aircraft, they also suggested to travelers that there was *no* airport or point of transition from ground to air. In the airport, passengers could feel as though they were already in an airplane sitting in wicker

Chafing under the restrictions of order, airports often manifest a type of horizontal violence, striking out at their own.

seats—already flying objects. One reading of this arrangement might suggest that flight was celebrated, while waiting on the ground was simply de-emphasized.

Yet as we saw with Fitzgerald's Cecelia, the contiguity runs in the other direction, too: flying in an airplane and traversing vast topographical expanses can all too easily feel similar to waiting in an airport—at rest in a geographical location, perhaps even painfully so. The time of waiting is collapsed into the time of flying; but the time of flying is equally collapsed into the time of waiting. Which is to say, airport seating exposes flying as simply another form of waiting, even though it may seem odd to describe it that way. To justify the dedication of resources, infrastructure, and ever-increasing pollution, flying must be understood as *purposeful* for free and active subjects. But in Fitzgerald's air travel in the 1930s and in the dual-purpose wicker seats of the 1920s, we discover that flight has been haunted by the sensation of flying objects sitting uncomfortably still: objects lingering—and not quite on purpose.

Lie flat in your massage seat

Temporal cessation around flight has hardly diminished; if anything, it is more apparent than ever—even with faster planes and an array of luxurious seating options for flying objects. Consider a web marketing campaign for Emirates Business

The omnipresence of airports is not incompatible with a certain humor, nor is it innocent of all passion.

Class, which displays a new media montage detailing what is supposed to be the apex of contemporary air travel. Elaborate slideshows and dramatically scored videos convey opulence and signify a continuous stream of consumer choices available to the high-end passenger qua flying object.

In the Dubai airport, before departure, Business Class passengers are invited to linger in the upper-level Emirates Terminal 3 Business Lounge, with its alluring row of cream-colored reclined seats. The Emirates website offers this poetic, elemental description of the Business Lounge:

> The interior design and seating areas—themed around the concepts of Fire, Water, Air and Earth—provide a soothing and enjoyable ambience. Relax and treat yourself to the range of premium services available for your pleasure. How you spend your journey in Business Class is up to you: lie flat in your massage seat, enjoy the wireless seat and entertainment control, use your own mini-bar and visit your exclusive onboard lounge. (Emirates)

Beyond the enveloping imperatives to "relax," "treat yourself," and "enjoy," I want to linger on another continuity—a continuity that appears once again between the passenger's specific comportment both on the ground and in the air. The flying object is encouraged to "lie flat." A short movie with a sensuous

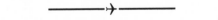

The airport's solitude is not the solitude of a person; it is the solitude of a system.

soundtrack demonstrates how one such passenger navigates his way through the reception area and to the reclined seats, where he rests before his flight . . . the video fading out as the passenger presumably slumbers into a tranquil preflight nap.

Of course at this point in the airport, the journey has not even really begun. Yet once aboard the Airbus A380 in the Business Class section of the plane, the passenger is interpellated into a strikingly similar position of rest. On the website, an interactive video sequence animates the reclining function of the Business Class flatbed.

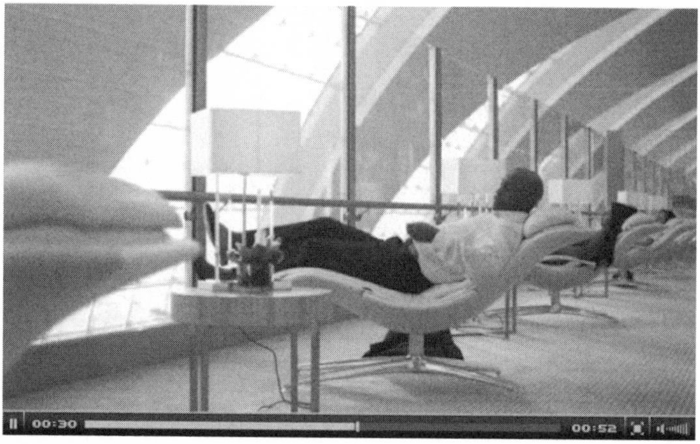

Figure 1 *Video still, Dubai Airport Business Lounge © 2012 Emirates.com.*

An articulated airport has an undecidable number of modes and sites where connections can be made.

Figure 2 *Video still, Business Class flatbed © 2012 Emirates.com.*

The angle of repose available to the Business Class passenger translates—or travels—from ground to air. Emirates advertises a standard of comfort—or an imperative to space-out—that is similarly achieved whether one is still at the airport, or hurtling through the air at 560 miles per hour. The flying object, lying still, can then proceed to kill time.

As in the earlier examples, Emirates's Business Class flatbed and the airport lounge chair compare the experiences of waiting on the ground and flying through the air. Emphasis is placed on repose,

I think of future airports. Much grossness will have evaporated. Things will have been scorched up, eliminated. There will be magic gates.

and present geographies are elided: the space of the airport can be tuned out as easily as the confines of the aircraft, or miles and miles of land or sea 43,000 feet below. The elimination of speed is dispersed, and sitting (or lying) still becomes the measure of flight.

These simple advertising injunctions to sit or lie back and relax in fact distort and even somewhat undermine the premise of *being there* on which flight is based: in such a uniformly reclined position, the human subject is quite literally rendered senseless and unconscious. Barthes's "motionless crisis of bodily consciousness" has reached its apotheosis—not in an especially cramped seat, but in a more luxurious class of travel, where the passenger is invited to "lie flat in your massage seat." And again, in these examples the elimination of speed is discovered to be operating both in the air *and* on the ground, in the airport when there is further time to sit still.

Hard architecture

In his book *Naked Airport: A Cultural History of the World's Most Revolutionary Structure*, Alastair Gordon claims that "airportness" emerged as a structure of feeling in the 1950s (170–71). According to Gordon, as flight became increasingly familiar to people, airports generated a new phenomenology of perception—at once geared toward jet flight and oriented

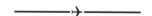

Is there a vista point from which to best perceive airports?

around thematically recognizable architectural and interior styles. Airports not only became increasingly inhabited places, but they also became places that people could experience as distinct *types* of space, geared toward flying objects. Arguably one of the most iconic symbols of airportness exists in the form of the Eames tandem sling seat by Herman Miller, which arrived on the scene in 1962 (Plate 3).

The Eames tandem was created to be a fashionable and spatially ingenious concept that would conjure the ambience of jet flight while accommodating masses of passengers waiting on the ground. Designed specifically for Chicago O'Hare International Airport, this modular form of group seating was layout-manipulable and scalable. As the Herman Miller website explains it, "The sleek look complements public spaces without overwhelming them." Human passengers are a constitutive object for the Eames tandem: as flying objects they justify, shape, and fill the spaces made by these seats.

The Eames tandem is of a class of furniture that comprises what the environmental psychologist Robert Sommer terms "hard architecture." These seats are structures that configure humans in such a way to discourage comfort, contemplation, and sociality. As Sommer describes such chairs,

> They seem deliberately designed to eliminate conversation among passengers. The seats are fastened together with

The wildest scenes at airports may become unaccountably familiar.

> armrests, clearly marking off each person's space; the rows are placed back-to-back or arranged classroom style facing the counter where the ticket agent plays the role of teacher. Another assumption is that all people are the same size and shape and therefore all chairs in an area should be identical. (75)

For Sommer such seating is indicative of social regress, noncommunication, and spatial tuning out—the effects of which are reflected in and felt across culture at large. Countless imitations of the Eames tandem have been installed throughout airports all over the world, and in popular culture the shape of such seats serves as a trope for annoying travel delays and the accompanying phenomenology of indefinite waiting.

Exemplifying this perspective is a memorable scene from Steven Spielberg's 2004 film *The Terminal*, in which Tom Hanks's airport-stranded character tries to sleep on generic Eames tandem seats, alternately falling through the cracks or getting jabbed by the unmovable armrests. This movie is about a drawn-out period of time in which a stateless character-object is quarantined to the terminal: his flight lands safely, but he cannot leave the airport—suggesting in another way an odd continuity between being in-flight and going nowhere on the ground. The generic airport seats echo the confined interior of an aircraft, and Hanks's contorted body recalls Cecelia's "Iron Maidens" in *The Last Tycoon*. In this scene we recognize the

Airports consist of the crash-mixing of bits of free-floating primordia, the stuff that makes up planes, bodies, and baggage.

time of the abject (or object) air traveler caught in the grip of hard architecture.

This scene in *The Terminal* draws from the same set of cultural associations as a passage from Don DeLillo's 1986 novel *White Noise*: "He was sprawled in the attitude of an air traveler, someone long since defeated by the stale waiting, the airport babble" (307). While Herman Miller originally designed the Eames tandem to merge seamlessly with the aesthetics and functional needs of air travel, it would seem that the culture of flight overdetermines the verisimilitude, and such seats are

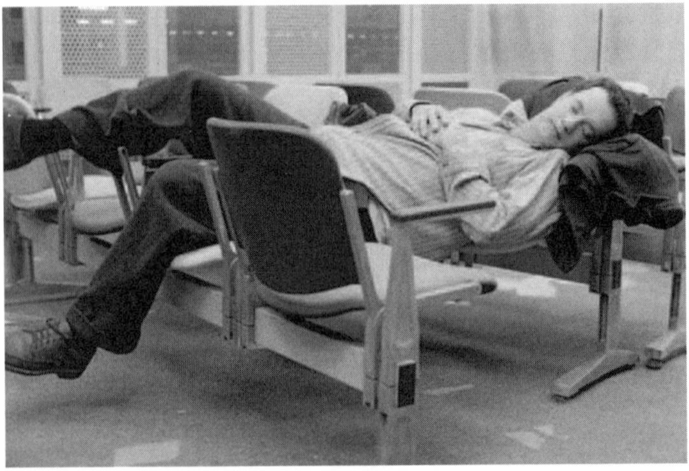

Figure 3 The Terminal *director Steven Spielberg © 2004 DreamWorks.*

Airports seemed to us at first only enigmatical transition zones for definite physical acts.

now ubiquitous reminders of the elimination of speed and the drawing out of time—whether on the ground or in the air, flying objects have to recline.

The continuity of seating between air travel and airport waiting was earlier hypostatized and satirized in Stanley Kubrick's *2001: A Space Odyssey* (1968). In this film, the humdrum experiences of commercial aviation were projected into space—in turn making space travel seem ordinary and banal. One scene takes place in an orbiting spaceport replete with a Hilton hotel, a face-time payphone of sorts, and a Howard Johnson's restaurant (Plate 4).

Standing out in this scene are the curvy red lounge chairs that conjure a futuristic landscape of flight while simultaneously insisting upon the old need for repose, for sitting still while soaring above ground. Hard architecture is softened here, but nonetheless results in a familiar schema where the leading edge of progress looks all too familiar, and flying objects recline in the old position of the air traveler turned jet-man. Kubrick's speculative future evokes the elimination of speed—the slow time of flight—as a present remainder, an enmeshed inconsistency that will not go away. It is no wonder that in *2001* flying objects are haunted by an inexplicable monolith: for what is progress when there is time to be killed?

It is with fragments such as these that we must do our best to make up a picture of the airport's life and character at this time.

"Dead time"

In his 1982 novel *The Names*, Don DeLillo formulates an elegant description of the phenomenology of air travel, which he sums up as the feeling of "dead time":

> This is time totally lost to us. We don't remember it. We take no sense impressions with us, no voices, none of the windy blast of aircraft on the tarmac, or the white noise of flight, or the hours waiting. Nothing sticks to us but smoke in our hair and clothes. It is dead time. It never happened until it happens again. Then it never happened. (7)

DeLillo's focus on the time of air travel reveals "hours of waiting" that get repeated day in and day out in the culture of flight. This time is a synesthetic eddy out of which nothing but "smoke" escapes. This is the time of Fitzgerald's Cecelia, and the time of Barthes's jet-man. It is the time of the Emirates Business Class traveler as well as the Economy Class airport-bound passenger trying to find a comfortable position on an Eames tandem or one of its many doppelgangers. This is the time of flying objects, sitting still.

Airlines commonly redirect passengers' attention from the "dead time" of air travel to spatial consolations, as in the United Airlines advertising campaigns for Economy Plus, a seating option wherein passengers can pay nominal fees for "up to five

Whoever lingers in airports and learns how to ask questions will have the experience that I had: a vast new panorama will open up before you.

extra inches of legroom" in the coach section of their aircraft. One early advertisement for Economy Plus that appeared on the back of boarding pass envelope jackets suggested that the space would be "leg roomier" (Plate 5).

In this image, United promises a spotlighted zone of pleasure reading while in-flight. The actual environment of air travel has vanished, and is exchanged instead for a wish image of solitary enjoyment—as if this is time that a flying object would *choose.* Nevertheless, the exaggerated attitude of recline combined with the focal point of this advertisement—the book—belies the "hours of waiting" that comprise "dead time." This is a time that confuses movement and stasis, ground and air, collective inhabitance of space and solipsistic spacing out.

The fantasy of isolation in the United Economy Plus advertisement piques an individualist meme that can represent bliss, as in the case of the happily relaxed airplane reader; but it is a meme that can equally result in existentialist dread—particularly when ensconced in the maddening confines of the airport. Flying objects are not always happy objects.

Time can stop completely

In the United States, federal regulations recently were passed to punish airlines for keeping passengers on aircraft for over three hours on the taxiway; but curiously it is the passenger stranded

The airport has been a fertile aesthetic category for the last one hundred years.

in the airport who enduringly represents a particularly tortured soul. Consider one *New Yorker* cartoon that appeared in the magazine in 2009.

This cartoon imagines Albert Einstein sitting in a prototypical airport departure lounge, his flaccid body in a familiar scrunched position, tired eyes staring blankly at nothing. The caption quips, "Einstein discovers that time can stop completely." In this image we can see crystalized the anxieties of flying objects and the imperative to sit at an awkward angle long before one's plane leaves the ground—if only in anticipation of more of the same, in flight.

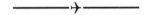

Figure 4 © *Warp/The* New Yorker *Collection/www.cartoonbank.com.*

Beside its congested gate areas and proletarian backrooms, the airport presents its informative text, rich in signs and meanings.

Here the elimination of speed is taken to its limit, with the airliner on the ground and no hints of a departure anytime soon: it is significant that the tarmac is vacant, with no workers, fuel trucks, or catering vans in sight. Jet travel, with its overt promise of an "excess of speed," has resulted in a state of repose prior to the plane. And as if to make sure we get the joke about hard architecture, Einstein even sits in a row of actual Eames tandem sling seats. This is "dead time" to such an extent that the great theorist of time is stymied by the mind-shattering temporal drag of everyday air travel, converted into an ironic flying object, sitting still, killing time. According to the cartoon, Einstein "discovers" this truth: it is as if a natural law is suddenly understood. Interestingly, Warp's depiction of Einstein syncs with another of Barthes's essays in *Mythologies*, "The Brain of Einstein," in which Barthes underscores the importance of "discovery" as a "magical essence" and a "basic element" (69). We thus see again a naturalization of the airborne subject, here via a "discovery" made by the paradigmatic scientist.

The anachronism of Einstein in the modern airport serves as an implicit layer of humor in the cartoon—yet it really raises another point of temporal confusion. Einstein died in 1955, while the cartoon is most likely intended to acquire its humor from the surge of staggering airport delays that have become new media events in recent years, and which are linked to terrorist threats,

The way we are disposed toward airports is nebulous, hard to define.

extreme weather patterns, and other global effects. Upon closer inspection, the anachronism grows less obvious.

First off, the airport architecture itself does not necessarily indicate an obvious anachronism, as the full viewing architectural tactics of floor-to-ceiling windows were well in effect by the mid-twentieth century. In his book *Airspaces* David Pascoe notes how in 1961 Paris's Orly airport was built to be "a window on the world, and a display case" (54). And as the media theorist Gillian Fuller has observed, historically "airports exult in a spectacle of outside" (164). These standards are hardly new features of airport design, then, and therefore Einstein's place in the departure lounge is not de facto jarring.

In the visible outside within the cartoon, the plane in the background appears to be a Boeing 737, which first went into service in 1968 and is one of the most widely used planes in service today. But the fuselage and wing design are general enough to call to mind the early 1950s, when jet airliners first entered the market. The Eames tandem chair, as we noted above, dates to 1962. On all these counts, then, placing Einstein in this airport delay is not that radical of a temporal discontiguity. But it is this ambiguous admixture of historical markers that reflects a reality principle accurate to flying objects: as if the project of time-saving, in fact, *dulls* temporal acuity. Furthermore, as we observed in *The Last Tycoon*, the boredom of airport waiting

Airports have no system and no proofs. But there is something like a logic of airports, the consistent sensibility which underlies them.

is hardly restricted to the contemporary traveler. On multiple points, then, the cartoon has almost a *timeless* quality.

For flying objects, time can stop completely—or seem recyclable across different and disparate historical moments. Indeed, it is Cecelia in *The Last Tycoon* who muses: "I suppose there has been nothing like airports since the days of the stage-stops—nothing quite as lonely, as somber-silent . . . airports lead you way back into history like oases, like the stops on the great trade routes" (14). Cecelia skips over more recent technological innovations in mobility (e.g., trains, cars) and relates air travel to another time entirely: the era of "stage-stops." The second figure is an odd simile—airport-as-oasis—which creates a double image, both an environmental mark (the fecund exception within an arid ecosystem) and a retrospective temporal gesture: the oasis calls to mind earlier times of travel and past modes of empire building.

Appropriately enough, a sort of oasis is part of the environmental ambience of Warp's cartoon: the minimal presence of a rolling tree line in the distant background of the image, at the edge of the airfield. Opposed to the stark and alienating grid of the airport, organic life goes on. One could speculate that it is precisely this subtle opposition that creates the comic tension in the cartoon: it is a perceived phenomenological abyss that separates the stale interior of the airport from vibrant

Stories about airports are makeshift things. They are composed of the world's debris.

life happening somewhere else, beyond the bounds of flying objects.

The flight took fifty minutes and seemed much longer

A scene in David Foster Wallace's posthumously published, unfinished novel *The Pale King* adds another piece to the airplane/airport seating puzzle. An early section of *The Pale King* concerns a character named Claude Sylvanshine who is en route to Peoria, Illinois, to take an accountancy exam. The following two sentences are the opening of the second chapter of *The Pale King*:

> From Midway Claude Sylvanshine then flew on something called Consolidated Thrust Regional Lines down to Peoria, a terrifying thirty-seater whose pilot had pimples at the back of his neck and reached back to pull a dingy fabric curtain over the cockpit and the beverage service consisted of a staggering girl underhanding you nuts while you chugged a Pepsi. Sylvanshine's window seat was in 8-something, an emergency row, beside an older lady with a sacklike chin who could not seem despite strenuous effort to open her nuts. (5)

In these lines we get an incredibly condensed picture of the haggard state of modern air travel and the flying objects

The airport is a place that is lost in the world.

contained therein. Quarters are close in the "terrifying thirty-seater"—a space that doubles as a frenzied cell of consumption, where Pepsi is "chugged." The apparent youngster who pulls the "dingy fabric curtain over the cockpit" reminds us of the late-stage development of the airplane pilot: far beyond Barthes's disillusioned jet-man, we're not even in a jet plane any more, and the pilot is exposed to be a barely concealed wage worker with acne. Flying objects, indeed.

The mention of Sylvanshine's specific seat on the aircraft marks a motif developed throughout the chapter. It is from Sylvanshine's cramped vantage point of semi-repose that *time* becomes a distinct part of this scenario, as the passage goes on to describe:

> The flight took fifty minutes and seemed much longer. There was nothing to do and nothing would hold still in his head in all the confined noise and after the nuts were gone there was nothing else for Sylvanshine to do to occupy his mind but try to look at the ground which appeared close enough that he could make out house colors and the types of different vehicles on the pale interstate the plane seemed to rock back and forth across. (6)

The elimination of speed thus becomes a matter of time, and specifically time to *kill*—for it is time that threatens to absorb

Sometimes the airport triumphs with a repulsive sneer while kneeling on the delayed traveler.

human agency completely. The view from the window seat becomes the merest modicum of entertainment for the strapped-in passenger Sylvanshine, sitting still, safely in flight—yet just on the edge of losing it. Sylvanshine feels the object-ness of his subjectivity acutely in the space/time of flight.

Wallace then makes recourse to familiar imagery at the end of this chapter, as Sylvanshine deplanes and pauses outside the aircraft:

> On the wet tarmac surrounded by restive breathers, turning 360° several times and trying to merge his own awareness with the panoramic vista, which except for airport-related items was uniformly featureless and old-coin gray and so remarkably flat that it was as if the earth here had been stamped on with some cosmic boot, visibility in all directions limited only by the horizon, which was the same general color of the sky and created the specular impression of being in the center of some huge and stagnant body of water, an oceanic impression so literally obliterating that Sylvanshine was cast or propelled back in on himself and felt again the edge of the shadow of the wing of Total Terror. (24)

Finally standing up, Sylvanshine turns around "several times" to view "the panoramic vista" which echoes the vague tree line in the Einstein cartoon, and Cecelia's "lonely," "somber-

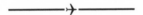

The airport is not a presence but is rather the simulacrum of a presence that dislocates, displaces, and refers beyond itself.

silent" airport-as-oasis. And like Stanley Kubrick's outer space imaginary in *2001*, feelings of cosmic alienation and of time at its end haunt Sylvanshine's airport impressions. Here once again, the passenger's position on the plane is placed on a continuum with a feeling of dread on the ground. Wallace shows how the extreme ends of this spectrum bend back onto one another: the bored and confined air traveler is eerily equated with the deplaned and grounded human subject. They are all flying objects, inescapably so. The problem of sitting in the culture of flight becomes a generalized problem about living in modern time.

In his book *Postmodernism, or, The Cultural Logic of Late Capitalism*, Fredric Jameson rightly notes how late capitalism tends toward "abstract and nonsituated" feelings, such as those evinced by "the anonymous space of airport terminals that all run together in your mind" (116).

Indeed, the big spaces of air travel have received much critical attention, from Marc Augé's seminal study *Non-Places: Introduction to an Anthropology of Supermodernity* to the recent book *Aerotropolis: The Way We'll Live Next*, by John D. Kasarda and Greg Lindsay. In the present book, I have attempted to focus on smaller spaces of flight—where and how travelers sit—in order to shift attention to matters of *time* and to the *objects* fliers become. The hyperaesthetics of air travel are imbricated with the seating fixtures that line the chambers of flight, and these

No one can tell the whole story of airports.

small spaces reveal profound temporal confusions. The seats of air travel are so easily passed over, so excruciatingly endured by flying objects, sitting still, killing time.

BAE 146

At some point along the way on any airport journey, the goal becomes to actually get on an airplane. Now it is time to turn to the planes that lie beyond the gates, connected and detachable, separate yet integral parts of airport life. Usually I am adamant that I'm not interested in airplanes, that my fascination with airports is really focused only inside the terminal, in the mundane passages of sitting around, standing in line, waiting for baggage, etc. But of course, the plane—as my old photographs show—is always part of the picture, always just a few steps away, the real object of flight.

In her 2012 novel *Contents May Have Shifted*, Pam Houston starts off one of the in-flight interchapters by narrating typical descent into the Kingdom of Bhutan; Houston describes the British Aerospace "146-100 STOL Regionals, jets famous for their tight turns and short landing and takeoff specs" (78).

This isn't the only thing the BAE 146 is known for. It's also known (to many ramp workers, anyway) for having a really tricky exterior lavatory dumping mechanism: the embedded

What would happen if airports were to incorporate a greater sense of the active vitality of foodstuff?

valve on the outside of the plane where you have to hook up a big black hose in order to evacuate the urine and feces collected over thousands of airborne miles.

I remember when I was trained to operate this type of valve: it was under the runway lights on the tarmac one summer night when our SkyWest aircraft were suddenly replaced by Air Wisconsin's jets—Air Wisconsin is another regional carrier for United Airlines. Air Wisconsin flew the BAE 146 planes at that time, and learning to park, clean, and prepare these unfamiliar jets for flight was like learning a new language. And the lavatory dump valve was like the subjunctive: full of its own nuances and hidden possibilities.

The lavatory cart is basically an enclosed reservoir of human waste on wheels; look out your window seat and you'll recognize it as a low-profile, squarish trailer with a big black tube like a snake coiled or curled kinkily around the top. At my airport, once a week a septic pump truck (the kind typically seen at campgrounds and servicing Port-a-Johns) would drive onto the tarmac and empty the cart. We would use the cart every evening (and sometimes between flights during the day) to empty out the toilets on the planes—when the crew would call in from fifteen minutes out, they might say they needed "lav service," which meant that it was time to haul out the lav cart and do our duty.

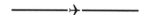

The airport is an amalgam of circuits, trajectories, and resistors.

Needless to say, it was not the preferred job among airline ramp workers. Despite the powerful aroma-canceling power of so-called "blue juice" (the admixture of chemicals inserted into the toilet to counteract the smell of waste), one might still encounter random spurts and sprays, or errant turds, while servicing the lav.

The lav cart has a six-inch diameter hose that hooks up to the side of the plane, and then there is a release lever on the plane that lets all the blue fecal matter and blue urine to travel down a loop-d-loop path into the reservoir. On the newer CRJs, this is a fairly neat and tidy task: the release lever is just to the side of the valve. When you're done, the valve simply flaps back and seals in place, and the separation of plane, poop, and person seems clear and distinct.

On the BAE 146, however, the release for the toilet chamber is actually located inside the valve itself, and basically you have to hook up the hose and then manipulate a spring-loaded interior rod to disengage the valve and get things flowing. At the end of the dump, you have to twist and push the rod just so to reinsert and seal the valve (which you cannot see, but must *feel* via the internal parts of the rod).

One of the first few times I did this, after I finished shaking the loose ends of blue toilet paper wads and dangling fecal matter into the reservoir on the lav cart, I looked up at the side of the

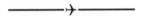

Airport dissidents are victims of the subtle machinations of a discrete social system.

plane and realized that the valve was missing: I was staring up into the underside abyss of the airplane toilet. I had not correctly reinserted the valve. I glanced in the hose—nothing. I looked around on the tarmac frantically, but to no avail. It was in the lav cart, somewhere in a foot-deep pool of shit, piss, and blue juice that had been stewing for a week—the septic truck was due to the airport the next day.

Luckily, the accouterments for this part of the job included gauntlet-style thick rubber gloves, and so I simply reached in, probed around with my fingers, swishing this way and that, around unknown clumps and viscera, until I found the metal valve. I fished it out, shook it off, and reinserted it in the side of the plane.

It was, for all intents and purposes, a close call. That plane could have been grounded for days—who knows where a replacement valve would have been located, and how long it would have taken for the airline to ship it up to Bozeman, Montana, using the inter-airline mail system? I remember that my coworker (who was busy dealing with lost baggage claims while I had started to clean the aircraft) nearly gagged when I described what had happened. For myself, I was more than a little thrilled by the whole experience. I had put my hand in that taboo nether region, that most abject place, where shit is collected and dealt with as if covertly, beyond the view of

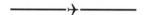

Contrary to popular belief, there is no easy generalization that can be made when it comes to airports.

thriving, bustling progress. I feel like I know the BAE 146, in a special way.

The BAE 146 is also the aircraft that by serendipity happens to appear in the background on the cover of my book *The Textual Life of Airports*.

When I flew through Paris in the fall of 2013, the sun rose across the tarmac as our Air France 777 taxied to the gate. As the golden orb lit up the gray expanse of concrete, I noticed in the distance a BAE 146 preparing for flight. I snapped a picture with my phone, and tweeted it to Pam Houston.

Figure 5 *BAE 146 in the background, cover photograph,* The Textual Life of Airports.

There are moments of surreal stillness in airports, and they are inescapable.

The BAE 146 is no longer in commercial service in the United States, and yet my own encounters with this aircraft continue to occur: in literature, in images, in lingering memories, in the stock photo adorning my book cover, even in old pictures I took and completely forgot about (Plate 6). I was somehow drawn to this plane (and jet bridges too, apparently—more on which shortly). Think of all the planes that we flew aboard just once, or perhaps several times, but that we are not likely to ever fly again. Where do planes go when they retire? How are we to chart their gradual arcs into decommission?

DC-9

Thirty-one miles northwest of Tucson, Arizona, over 100 retired commercial airliners rest in the desert—fuselages and engines in the gradual process of being scrapped, refurbished, or sealed up for uncertain futures (Plate 7).

The Pinal Airpark is home of Marana Aerospace Solutions, a company that acquires, stores, and services commercial airliners. They specialize in "heavy maintenance, storage and parking, component repair and overhaul, painting and exterior detail, and end-of-life solutions." The latter is particularly poignant as one roves across the terrain on Google's satellite view, gazing down at the angular rows of retired jetliners. This is one of

The boundary between physical and nonphysical is very imprecise for airports.

the notorious airplane "boneyards" that dot the deserts of the American Southwest.

Many of the smaller airliners, some nestled together nose-to-wing and recognizable by their occasional red tops, are McDonnell Douglas DC-9s adorned with the now obsolete livery of Northwest Airlines. This model first flew in 1965, and the last DC-9, the 976th, was manufactured in 1982. Northwest operated these planes regularly until 2008, when the airline was absorbed by Delta and the DC-9s were decommissioned and sent to Pinal Airpark.

Looking down from the simulated satellite camera's eye on my laptop screen, I'm confronted with the uncanny realization that I most likely spent hours in several of those aircraft now parked in the desert. I flew Northwest regularly in the late 1990s and early 2000s, and I recall well the near-ear thrum of the tail-mounted Pratt & Whitney JT8D turbofan engines from the farthest-to-the-back seats. I also watched these planes on the tarmac in Bozeman (recall Plate 2).

Among a host of other pragmatic advantages, the tail-mounted engines on these aircraft simplified the wing design and made the DC-9s versatile planes able to take off and land on short runways and thereby service smaller airports as well as major hubs. These planes were attuned to geography from the outset, anticipating the range of locations that the airliner could

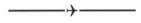

Choice in an airport is a gloomy thing.

reach. In spite of a long and fairly successful life in commercial service, the DC-9 now finds itself outmoded by newer and more efficient aircraft.

Still, the DC-9 is not quite history. In 2012, it served as the campaign plane for vice presidential hopeful Paul Ryan, and was frequently visible in the background as Ryan alighted in towns across the Unites States, waving vigorously from the air-stairs.

The campaign plane's temporary livery urged taxiway constituents to "Believe in America." Partisan politics aside, this adage might be applied in earnest to the plane itself: the slogan becomes *almost* endorsable when we consider a family of aircraft built over thirty years ago and flown consistently, one punishing flight after another, day in and day out, and still occasionally churning the sky. Even in the face of its visible decline—as evinced by the desert layout of retired Northwest DC-9s—the aircraft's tenacity is impressive. The DC-9 is the smaller and older cousin to the MD-80, which remains in regular service with many airlines today, and which served as Mitt Romney's own campaign plane.

The DC-9s in the desert, awaiting service, scrap, or sale, exist almost at the level of abstraction: they are objects with histories, but objects which have been taken out of use, and exist, like the sculpted fragments of Shelley's "Ozymandias," as indices of other times. Likewise, the Northwest Airlines' logos and color

The imaginary of the airport is neither true nor false, it is a deterrence machine set up in order to rejuvenate the fiction of the real.

schemes communicate in a sandy void a no-longer extant brand, corporate semiotics rendered obsolete.

As for the actual Romney campaign planes, the particular DC-9 and MD-83 decked out with the plushest seating and promises of a better America—these planes have now been thoroughly cleaned and by Active Aero, the company that leases them. These two planes, old and well worn, are most likely flying today—shuttling sports teams or rock bands around the globe. Meanwhile, their factory-born siblings rest in the desert, offering themselves up as spare parts and still satellite views.

Boeing 737

Around the same time the first DC-9 took off, Boeing was developing the 737. This aircraft entered airline service in 1968, and will be familiar today to anyone who has flown Southwest Airlines; the 737 is the only plane model Southwest operates, and with its noticeably bold pain job the plane is an integral part of the airline's corporate identity (Plate 8). Look up next time you hear a faint roar in the sky, and if you see a red-belly blue plane, it's mostly likely a Southwest Airlines 737.

The most notable difference from the DC-9 is in the 737's wing-mounted engines. If the DC-9's tail-mounted engines were a result of geographical awareness and flexibility, the wing-

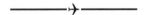

Airports always find themselves somewhere between fine art and kitsch.

mounted engines of the 737 indicate a differently grounded consciousness, a mindfulness of the maintenance required by such a transportation workhorse. These engines are easier to access and repair, suggesting a focus on keeping the aircraft in the skies as much as possible.

Unlike the DC-9, which is approaching extinction and a near archaeological status, the 737 is the most widely flown and robustly produced aircraft today, with 8,305 built as of fall 2014. Another 4,218 of the aircraft are on order from Boeing and in various stages of production. As if to make these numbers real, the sage Wikipedia offers this astounding factoid concerning the 737: "There are, on average, 1,250 Boeing 737s airborne at any given time, with two departing or landing somewhere every five seconds." Pause for a moment to imagine one of these airliners departing, and another landing; now consider this as an unceasing cycle.

Still, the 737 aircraft is not above mortal strife. The reader might well recall an incident that took place in April, 2011, when Southwest Airlines Flight 812 experienced a six-foot fuselage tear mid-flight, resulting in depressurization and an emergency landing. The cause was determined to be "preexisting fatigue"—in other words, stress on the aircraft's skin after years of grueling daily use.

There is no fixity in airports: they can come in to being, alter, disintegrate, disappear completely.

One photograph snapped after the incident revealed an extra layer of intrigue. The picture arguably reflects an innocent and spontaneous interest in the materiality of the damaged plane: it's a simple blurry snapshot from the vantage point of a likely surprised passenger, standing a row behind another passenger snapping a picture of the actual ceiling tear. Yet then this photo also suggests interest in *capturing* a digital image of this materiality—indeed, in capturing a digital image *being captured* of this materiality. The occasion was one not only for seeing how a plane is actually constructed, then, but as well for redoubling and disseminating such a view-being-taken. The picture reflects our fascination with the proliferation of digital photography on airplanes.

Of course everything migrates online these days, so in one respect there might be nothing surprising about the Southwest 737 ceiling tear ending up as a new media bit. But we really must linger on how odd this image is: the picture is as much about taking an iPhone photo as it is about representing the damaged airliner.

As if to compound this issue, the way "The Southwest Experience" has been marketed, it appears to be as much about being online as it is an experience of actual flight. Consider the airline's infographic that explains how the customer/passenger is to navigate said experience (Plate 9). The Boeing 737, and by metonymic extension the traveler in flight, is nestled into a new media chain of loosely affiliated object-actions: computer

The airport tears one to pieces, and each fresh wave of consciousness is poison.

mouse, shopping cart, airport sign, boarding passes, 737 airliner, social media icons. The most widely flown aircraft is shown to be another mere unit of contemporary life, juxtaposed with surfing the web, disposable paper products, passing a familiar green sign on the highway, and thumbing a smartphone.

After the ceiling tear incident, the Federal Aviation Administration swiftly called for regular inspections of the lap joints on certain 737 airframes that had flown over 30,000 cycles, and a widespread crisis was averted. But I remember flying on Southwest to visit my in-laws a month or so after the widely reported ceiling tear: I held my then eighteen-month-old son on my lap as the plane lifted off the ground, vaguely wondering whether I'd be able to cling to him tightly enough in the event that the fuselage above me came undone at cruising altitude. Such in-flight paranoia aside, the 737 is not threatened by wear-and-tear so much as it risks being de-emphasized (if not exactly outmoded) by a tangential, emergent sensibility, an alien notion of travel. As the Southwest Experience info-graphic insinuates by its first and last symbols, more and more, we go places on screens, too.

Dreamliner

Boeing's latest airliner, the 787, is also known as the Dreamliner. This aircraft promises larger windows, a slick new toilet with a hand-motion sensor for flushing, ambient lighting, and better air quality in the cabin—such features are all on the inside, for passengers to enjoy.

In an article titled "Test Flying the 787 Dreamliner," the *New York Times* called it "a plane of the future"—yet on first glance it might not appear all that different from planes we have seen before. The two features most visibly different on the exterior of the aircraft—viewable up close thanks to Wikimedia Commons—are the noise-reducing chevrons on the engine nacelles, and the raked wingtips to decrease drag (Plate 10). But these are subtle aspects, noticeable perhaps only to aviation geeks.

Early promotional coverage of the plane's entry into service hyped the atmospheric improvements and minor tweaks to the Dreamliner's passenger experience; but the earliest images of this experience looked all too common: cramped seats, narrow aisles, stuffed overhead bins—and among passengers, the recognizable, slouched attitude that comes with waiting to disembark or deplane. As if to underscore this sense of familiarity, the *New York Times* reporter Stephanie Rosenbloom put it succinctly this way: "Even occasional fliers will find themselves on Dreamliners in the coming years." A plane of the future thus flies into the friendly skies of banality.

In terms of the aircraft's design, however, the Dreamliner reimagines how an airliner's body can be made, with "one-piece

Turning and turning in the widening gyre, the airport worker cannot hear the airplane.

composite barrel construction" that forgoes traditional aluminum skin sheets for sandwiched and bonded lightweight materials that make pressurization more efficient and cut fuel costs.

After the aircraft first entered service in late 2011, it was plagued by minor impediments including electrical fires and fuel spills. These malfunctions were referred to as "teething problems," as if to imply that the airplane is a living thing—indeed, an infant (in the *New York Times*, "Fuel Leak Is Latest Setback for Boeing's Dreamliner"). Boeing was quick to point out that all new planes have issues as they enter service, and that the number of 787 problems is in fact on par with the problems the Boeing 777 had at the beginning of its life, in 1995. (The 777 has since undergone its own rough patch, if for less consistent reasons.) If prospective passengers were alarmed by the profusion of headlines about the Dreamliner's problems, they might also consider that this is the fate of a new airplane in our new media ecology: no other new airliner has had to brave the viral communicative environment of the internet.

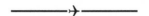

The Dreamliner is also a "new media" aircraft in a plainer sense, as a vessel for passenger USB ports, personal touchscreens, LED ambient lighting, and individually dimming windows. Looking deeper inside the aircraft, we find yet another familiar new media component: the lithium-ion batteries that power the aircraft's APU (basically an internal generator that starts the turbofans) as well as the cockpit's electrical system. These batteries were the source of compounding problems for the aircraft, and the Dreamliner was grounded worldwide for a period of months, due to overheating batteries and the notorious specter of "smoke in the cockpit" (*The New York Times*, "Regulators Around the Globe Ground Boeing 787s"). Lithium-ion batteries are mundane if somewhat invisible, tucked inside cell phones and laptop computers. They charge quickly and hold a lot of juice, but they tend to overheat. Who hasn't felt an iPhone get ridiculously hot in their pocket once or twice? This oft-cited comparison reveals further the weird continuum—between wide-body airliner and handheld device—across which the Dreamliner seems to slide.

The Dreamliner represents a crisis point of sorts. It hovers between that which can be grasped, and something verging on a "hyperobject," or a thing that is too spread out across time and space for humans to quite comprehend (à la Timothy Morton's articulation of the term). The Dreamliner is an airliner like the twentieth-century DC-9, and yet it beckons us into a twenty-first-century future of economy and efficiency. The Dreamliner promises a personal utopia of new media pleasures, bundled together with the surges and swells of consistent and collective transit lines. The Dreamliner is the same, but different.

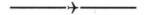

Today airports do not develop slowly and succeed each other gradually, but instead succeed one another so rapidly as to give travelers no breathing space to prepare.

It is too early to know whether the Dreamliner's battery problems will reemerge and threaten again, possibly becoming insurmountable and causing the aircraft to buckle as a truly innovative program; or whether the Dreamliner will grow out these teething pains and become as successful and ubiquitous as the 737 is today. By Boeing's projected sales of 5,000 Dreamliners over the next twenty years, it would seem for now that the latter will be the case. Dreamlining could become as common as, well, dreaming.

But I can't help but contemplate how first the 737s, and then the Dreamliners, too, will end up in airplane boneyards—if not very soon, then some twenty, thirty, forty, or fifty years from now, when their systems and designs are exhausted, when we need new dreams.

Weather

When I worked at the airport, the conditions on the tarmac could be intense: massive snowdrifts or treacherous ice around the plane in the winter, cannonading thunderstorms that rolled off the Bridger Range and onto the scorching concrete in the summer.

The Big Sky always presented some possibility of interference: natural events that could throw off the day's scheduled flights,

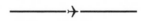

It can never be satisfied, the airport, never.

often with repercussions that would last for days, making for long hours at the computers rescheduling irate passengers.

At the other end of our routes, we were also constantly aware of the fluctuating storm cells off the Front Range that bombarded Denver International Airport nearly every afternoon. I recall again the time after that massive hailstorm in Denver, when our CRJ arrived with hundreds of tiny dimples all over its wings—weather scars. The jets barraged by hailstones should not have been flying, according to our operation manuals—but life had to go on, the passengers were waiting, and so someone somewhere had given the go ahead for the battered planes to fly.

Usually, though, we experience airport weather at a remove, from window seats looking out, the interior noises of our aircraft muffling the elements, perhaps a few raindrops streaking across the glass.

Another way we experience weather in airports comes through informational displays, streamed data in small type, miniature graphics, and semiotic cues—such as when the self-check-in kiosk tells me that it is 42 degrees at my destination airport of Traverse City, Michigan, and cloudy, communicated through a tiny icon of clustered cumuli hovering on the glowing blue screen. Here, airport weather is embedded within an elaborate matrix of logistics including gate information,

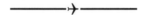

Airports are above all an attitude of mind and an expression of the will to dominate.

boarding time, and instructions to upgrade and print my seating assignment. The weather is one factor among so many options and data points—and yet it also floats in its own almost transcendent realm, something beyond the scope of the procedural operations of air travel.

The official language in the contract of carriage for most airlines lumps weather under the broad category of "conditions beyond control"—in other words, situations that the airlines are not liable for in the event that flights are delayed or canceled. It is a common enough experience to have an airline representative play the "weather" card, by way of not having to explain or compensate for a missed flight, protracted delay, or unintended night in a sketchy and exorbitantly priced airport hotel.

Airport weather seems obvious, something to be avoided or at the very least skirted: an ethereal potential that lurks at the periphery of every traveler's trip, and which occasionally becomes an all-encompassing, tyrannical center point. But I wonder about the obviousness of this matter of contingency.

I started to think more about this topic after my son Julien received Richard Scarry's classic children's book *A Day at the Airport* as a gift, and we went on a binge of reading the book every night for several weeks in a row. The book is all about airport weather.

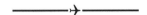

Always in formation, airports trudge on through each night and day, sensitive yet oblivious.

The opening pages find Huckle and Sally Cat out for a day of sailing. But just as they get under way it begins to rain, and Father Cat tells Huckle and Sally, "There's nothing to do but to go back home." The page then editorializes, beyond the persona of any visible character, "What a disappointment." This is a common enough sentiment in children's books, noticeable also in Dr. Seuss's classic *The Cat in the Hat*, where another Sally is subject to bad weather:

The sun did not shine
It was too wet to play.
So we sat in the house
All that cold, cold, wet day.

Where Dr. Seuss uses this prompt as a way to introduce the eponymous feline troublemaker, Richard Scarry comes up with another solution to the rainy day doldrums. On their way home, the cat family stops at Scotty's filling station for gas, and there they meet Rudolf Von Flugel, who comes up with a new idea for Huckle and Sally, and suggests this idea to Father Cat: "Why don't they come with me? I'm going to the airport. There's lots to see there, even when it rains!" The airport is staged as an escape from the rain, but also as a kind of exception *from* the bad weather: at the airport, life goes on, independent of weather.

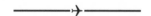

Airports make civilization impossible with all their charm, all their silliness.

But there's something a little off on these pages: Rudolf is driving his "airplane car" (a converted propeller plane that drives backward), and there are also small biplanes that appear to be landing on top of Scotty's gas pump bay. The subject of flight is already in the air.

A Day at the Airport proceeds to trot through all the familiar and sometimes unfamiliar operations of everyday commercial flight . . . and always with the looming low presence of the heavy rainclouds at the top of the page. It's a book about airports, but also a book about *weather*, and in particular the ways that airports *frame* weather, or make it perceptible and navigable as such. And just as the airport frames the weather, the weather also brings an unexpected function of the airport into focus: it's a place for *play*, for things to happen—thus the story is riddled with all sorts of things going awry, as cars hurtle off the parking garage, suitcases flop open all over the tarmac, and the perennially clumsy Mr. Frumble chases his errant hat around, eventually transgressing the as-if secure side of the airport and ending up on the runway ("No running on the runway!").

So, one aspect of airport weather might be *play*: weather is that ever-present point of slippage, of integral looseness wherein the airport's strict functionality goes out the window, and things slide in ways that cannot always be prepared for—but might be played *with*.

If you listen to the faintest but constant suggestions of the airport, you will see to what extremes, even to insanity, it may lead you.

Now let us leave the playful pages of Richard Scarry, and move on to another text, a more recognizably literary and even environmental one. The nature writer Barry Lopez's short story "Pearyland" begins at the airport, with a drawn-out disclaimer of sorts:

> I apologize for not being able to tell you the whole of this story. It begins at the airport at Søndre Strømfjord in Greenland and it happened to a man named Edward Bowman. . . .
>
> About a hundred of us were waiting around for planes, his out to Copenhagen, with Søndre Strømfjord socked in. He'd been at the airport for six days; I'd been there just a few, with four Inuit friends from Clyde Inlet, on Baffin Island. . . .
>
> We were all standing by, long hours at the airport. Some people went into town, but the notion that the weather might suddenly clear for just a few minutes and a plane take off kept most of us around, sleeping in the lounges, eating at the restaurant, using the phones. (62)

"Pearyland" unfolds as a story quilted with ecology and spirituality. It is the tale of a *taphonomist* who, when he ventures to the far north to study how animals get recycled into the soil, discovers that there is a vaguely religious function to this process: animals that aren't prayed for after their deaths don't get new

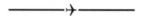

Airports rest in silence, uncommunicative; they rest in the extreme obscurity of human relationships.

bodies. Bowman has landed in a sort of purgatory where animal bodies without souls linger. Lopez's story is haunting and deftly told, and its innuendoes about reincarnation might very well be worth heeding, in spite of their ambiguous quality.

In fact it is precisely this ambiguity that interests me: the rationale for Lopez's incomplete, hazy story is housed in the airport, or rather in an airport delay. The narrator receives only part of the story, and before it can end in any fully satisfying way, the weather suddenly clears and Bowman's plane departs. "Pearyland" is a product of airport weather, a narrative fragment justified by its structural components. Thus another thing about airports that weather exposes is a degree of *indeterminacy*. When fog settles heavy over the runways, or when hail pelts and dents the wings and fuselage of planes, the indeterminate status of things is exposed—the fabric isn't quite so seamless, aerodynamic surfaces are marred, and stories can get interrupted and become ambiguous. As much as these spaces depend on strict schedules, careful predictions, and secure borders, airports also revel in the contingencies of weather: the arrested journey, the punctuated or obscured landscape, the story that is both made possible by dense fog and cut short by its sudden lifting.

The second chapter of David Foster Wallace's unfinished novel *The Pale King* lends another fragment to the airport weather imaginary. In this section, recall, we meet the hyperaware

The interpretation of airports is peculiar, and hardly proper to philosophy.

character Claude Sylvanshine, a "fact psychic," who is en route to Peoria, Illinois, to take his CPA exam. As we learned in "Seats," above, Sylvanshine is introduced while onboard a fifty-minute commuter flight from Chicago to Peoria, Illinois, and his observations from his cramped seat amount to a scathing critique of the culture of flight (and perhaps late capitalism in general). We've seen how Wallace indicts the airplane seat. Most useful for our interests here, though, are some passages toward the end of the section, as Sylvanshine's mundane journey comes to a close:

> They deplaned and descended and collected the carry-on bags that had been confiscated and tagged at Midway and now rested in a motley row on the wet tarmac beside the airplane, and stood then briefly en masse on a complexly painted cement expanse while someone with orange earmuffs and clipboard counted them and then crosschecked with a previous count undertaken at Midway. The whole operation seemed somewhat ad hoc and slapdash. . . .
>
> The wind was warm and steamy. A large hose extended from a small truck to the commuter plane's stomach and appeared to be refueling the craft for its turnaround to Chicago. Up and back again and again all day. There was a strong scent of fuel and wet cement. (20)

A force of rupture is integrally tied to airports.

This section in Wallace's story is about an utterly unremarkable trip, an ordinary adventure that goes off without a hitch—and yet which is haunted by a vague sense of being "ad hoc and slapdash." The bland weather here—"The wind was warm and steamy"—functions as a curious remark on the bland "operation" as a whole. It is something that has no charm, no magic, no drama. Or rather, all the drama is *internal*, perhaps even *latent*—like the stuff that lurks beneath dreams, for Freud. Earlier in the chapter, Sylvanshine notes small raindrops beading on the aircraft window, as the plane rocks back and forth above a superhighway.

Wallace embeds a kind of eerie existential dread just beneath the veneer of a humdrum commuter flight, wherein everything is operating more or less normally, and yet it's also all a little freaky, including the unremarkable weather that is nevertheless noted. Wallace reminds us how airport weather is supposed to be *unnoticeable*, and should fade into the muted background of a normal travel day (or night). But the normal atmosphere of flight itself can become weirdly heavy, inducing strange perceptions and even a kind of overwhelming terror. Airport weather isn't just about the weather. It's about a whole swarm of actions and things taking place in this manufactured landscape. For Wallace, the dreary airport tarmac scene finally swerves into a profound awareness of a paradox: the centered, hyperconscious human being teeters on the edge of cosmic indifference and oblivion.

An examination of the structure and operation of airports quickly reveals that they can barely tolerate the concept of travel.

Is airport weather the always-looming threshold of modern progress? Is this the end of airports?

The anthropologist Kathleen Stewart, in her form-defying book *Ordinary Affects*, uses a scene spawned by airport weather as an example of an ordinary "contact zone for analysis" (5). Stewart's larger project in this book is to map the routine yet haunting surface of interactions and tension points that play out in contemporary American culture, enacting a heuristic for recording and gauging what she calls "ordinary affects."

In the section "A Raindrop Falls in Houston," Stewart describes a routine flight to Austin via Houston, which gets interrupted when "the pilot announces that there has been heavy rain in the Houston area. The new air traffic control tower has flooded (there's a flaw in the design), and they have shut down the airport. Her plane is short on fuel, so it's diverted to Austin" (89). But in a Kafkaesque accumulation of technicalities and elaborate structural contradictions, Stewart is not able to leave the plane in Austin (her actual destination), and instead must sit on the plane for nine hours on the runway, after which point she is flown back to Houston, only then to face an abject layover and seemingly endless lines at the airport the next day, the ripple effect of mass cancelations. At one point during the initial botched reroute, Stewart reports, "The pilot announces that there is no plan" (90). Stewart closes the case study this way: "The next morning the

---

What is put into question by airports is precisely the quest for a rightful beginning, an absolute point of departure.

news reports that Houston airport is back to normal, and we try to forget, as if nothing happened. Just move on" (90).

For Stewart, airport weather seems to promise nothing less than a kind of radical break in progress, *for the sake of progress.* Airport protocols around weather spark a surge of sheer irrationality; yet it is a surge that, with rather minimal effort, can be forgotten and absorbed back into the mainstream. Conditions beyond control have a way of infiltrating and infecting the most mundane and normally functional routines of flight, and these infiltrations and infections must then be dynamically repressed or smoothed over.

And now a Houston story of my own, an anecdote triggered by a photograph I snapped on my iPhone as I was flying back home to New Orleans from Boston, in January 2013 (Plate 11). I had hoped to catch a glimpse of the new Boeing Dreamliner on my trip, and sure enough, as I was racing to make my connection in Houston, I spotted a United Airlines Dreamliner preparing for departure. Taking a quick detour, I shot down an escalator and sprinted down the concourse in time to see the pushback and hear the low revving thrum of the unfamiliar engines, and to watch the Dreamliner lumber off toward the runway.

It was an ordinary day of travel, with no delays or threatening weather to speak of. The blandness of the scene was complete; and yet there was room to play, both in terms of the gathering

What constitutes the airport is a site of massive contestation, played out across millions of minor journeys.

clouds, and in my own ability to take advantage of a few minutes between flights to view a spectacle. Little did I know then, nor could I have known, the indeterminacy brewing in the Dreamliner itself, whose batteries were beginning to fail around the world, catching fire, sending smoke into cockpits, and resulting in a wholesale grounding of the planes at great cost to Boeing and the airlines operating the planes. And here, the climate of air travel in general exposed a deep absurdity, wherein the Dreamliner battery packs would be fixed so as to not overheat, but would also be equipped with titanium vents in the event of unforeseen overheating. The cause of the Dreamliner battery fires remains something of a mystery—and yet the planes are back in the air, braving and redoubling conditions beyond control.

With this closing story I've attempted to zoom way out, so that airport weather no longer just means precipitation, temperature, and wind. It's the electricity and currents that run through all aspects of air travel. It's the fun and the danger, it's the stories and drama, the storms and the calm, the frame and the focus.

Jet Bridges

The romance of flight is often associated with the dramatic landscape of tarmac and runways, where we encounter airport

Stripped of remembrance, the airport displays its strength.

weather as planes prepare to take off. Humphrey Bogart and Ingrid Bergman say their last words to each other in a weird foggy glow on the taxiway in the closing minutes of *Casablanca*. A Lockheed 12 aircraft looms behind them, promising adventure. This is a threshold of escape—a point of departure for the characters, an apt space of closure for the film. Woody Allen paid homage to this scene—if also making it the subject of postmodern pastiche—in his 1972 film *Play It Again, Sam*, recast with Diane Keaton and Woody Allen, and a modern San Francisco International Airport standing in for the exotic airfield of *Casablanca* (Plate 12).

When I worked at the airport, the tarmac still pulsed vividly with romance prior to boarding. After passengers gave their boarding passes to agents like me, they would trundle down two flights of stairs that then emptied onto the windswept asphalt, our CRJ waiting for them fifty feet away, gleaming in the sunlight. Ramp workers in oversize fluorescent vests were positioned on the tarmac to guide the passengers toward the aircraft's door-stairs, and to prohibit errant passengers from suddenly sprinting across the open expanse. There was something about the sight of passengers staggering out to the plane, in all types of weather and against the steady whine of the jet's APU, which brought a spirit of adventure to this utterly routine practice.

The alienation introduced by airports is not something you can ever really get away from.

But perhaps a different sort of charm emerges with "the disappearance of the staircase in favor of safer, more weatherproof indoor jet bridges"—this quote comes from an online article called "How Convenient Jetways Helped Kill Airline Glamour." When I worked at the Bozeman airport, Northwest and Delta had the only two jet bridges, installed for the larger Airbuses and 737s that flew to Minneapolis and Salt Lake City. Our smaller jets, bound for Denver, could be efficiently accessed and serviced on the apron in what is called a "hardstand." (Horizon Airlines was in the same boat as us, with their small Dash 8 regional planes that hopped over the Cascades to and from Seattle several times a day.)

During the second year of my tenure at the airport, construction had begun on a new jet bridge for our United flights. A laconic French-Canadian crew set up shop on the tarmac and started to work on this strange new growth, a long metal tentacle dangling off the old familiar terminal corner. When the jet bridge was complete, I learned how to maneuver it on its jerky pivoted arc; how to extend and retract the tunnel; and how to project the accordioned flexion of the weather canopy over the top of the aircraft. There was a shrill Klaxon that went off intermittently whenever the jet bridge's main power was turned on; this caused an eerie ambience of emergency to hover around the tarmac, even when nothing was wrong. I learned about the auto-leveler,

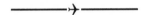

The airport will always resist you, in some way or another.

that little rubber-edged disc that hangs over the edge of the jet bridge and touches the plane: as the plane fills with passengers and luggage, and so gets heavier, the disc turns ever so gradually, keeping the jet bridge level with the plane.

Because our planes were regional jets, we actually had to use a small metal bridge designed to fill the gap between the jet bridge and the small plane—so, a miniature jet bridge that extended the jet bridge. This required an extra stage of training that was quite nerve-wracking, for the heavy connector was cumbersome and sharp-edged, and could easily damage the fuselage if jostled or hastily set up.

Then there was the new mayhem of the last-second gate-checked carry-on bags, an everyday micro-drama that seasoned travelers know so well. A small elevator with a two-shelf cart waited in the jet bridge, for those bags that would not fit in the undersize overhead bins on the scaled-down aircraft. Passengers deposited these bags (often uncertainly) on the cart on their way down the jet bridge; it would then be lowered to the tarmac after the last passengers boarded. As ramp workers, we perpetually had our pockets full of those neon tags that say "Gate Check" or some such phrase, which we attached at the last second to people's roller bags and many-strapped backpacks, signaling to our compatriots in Denver to yank these bags off first and hustle them up to the jet bridge as the passengers deplaned. (Larger

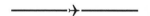

Airports are not neutral. We are inside them, and they are inside us.

airports attach plastic chutes to their jet bridges, down which slide strollers, children's car seats, and other gate-checked things to the baggage handlers below.)

I can still conjure the clanging vibrations of the metal stairs that lead down from the jet bridge to the tarmac, the empty thud of its floor as I sprinted down from the boarding area to check with the flight crew to see if they were ready for their passengers. I recall the lilt of the carry-on cart and the awkward angle of pull required so that it wouldn't clip my ankles or spin out of control near the plane. The jet bridge is rife with so many low-tech moments—when all the elaborate communication systems must be assisted by face-to-face affirmation, when the precision of jet flight is aided by wobbly plastic wheels, simple inclines, and human muscle power.

Reminiscing, I recently looked down on the Bozeman airport from the satellite view on Google Maps. I noticed that the terminal now has several more jet bridges hanging off of it. Free-range tarmac boarding and deplaning looks to have become a thing of the past at this airport, another myth of the Wild West rendered obsolete.

It's doubly ironic that Woody Allen used SFO to echo the famous tarmac scene from *Casablanca*, since by 1972 airports were well into the jet age, with bridges outmoding tarmac boarding. In fact, SFO was the first airport in the country to

There is an urgent need to develop radical perspectives on airports.

install jet bridges, in 1959. However, plenty of airports *still* board their aircraft in the original crude way, passengers schlepping across the blasted asphalt on the way to their planes. These two forms of boarding coexist, but tarmac boarding has become but a signal of regional esotericism or infrastructural destitution, rather than a necessary and seductive encounter with the hot, loud realities of air travel.

It may sound like a minor matter among the more pressing concerns of safety and security, new aircraft systems, and airline mergers over the past fifty years. Running to catch a connection, no one laments finding a jet bridge upon arriving. Today, that familiarity and expectation has made the jet bridge disappear into the background, an unconsidered if vaguely necessary space. But like the smartphone touchscreens its passengers fondle while queued up inside it, the jet bridge is hardly a transparent interface. It shapes our experiences of flight.

What is this thing? A jet bridge is a machine attached to a building, a machine that connects another machine (the airplane) to the structure of the airport itself. A jet bridge is part of an airport, but it also extends the airport, supplements it. It guides movement and facilitates the efficient loading and unloading of passenger aircraft. It is a passage, a narrow hallway. Sometimes it can be quite long and labyrinthine feeling—even when you know exactly where it begins and ends. It can feel

But this is the final question: how many of us really believe in airports?

old school and well worn, adorned with retro color palates and classic aviation motifs; or it can be sleek and new, plastered with the latest promotional materials for platinum credit cards and elite frequent-flier programs.

In some ways, a jet bridge is the most concentrated form of an airport, the purest interstitial zone that mediates your leap into the sky. It shines with utter simplicity and directness, perhaps at the beginning of a long-awaited trip; or it can lead to an onslaught of existential horror, such as when boarding is taking too long and the hundred-degree heat outside seeps in, suffocating. Conversely, a jet bridge can be a brutally frigid ice cave, shattering the fantasies of climate control so carefully maintained by airport concourses and aircraft cabins.

A jet bridge can seem ominous or inviting, a point of departure or a point of no return. Paul Thomas Anderson riffed on this ambiguity in a pivotal scene of the 2003 film *Punch Drunk Love*, when Adam Sandler's sheltered and volatile character Barry lopes down the jet bridge in a protracted slow motion shot, lumbering into an uncertain future beyond, as if this act will change the character's fate forever (Plate 13). In *Punch Drunk Love* the jet bridge is an overdetermined vehicle for character development: we see that he's going somewhere, all right—even if it is just down a dank tunnel to a waiting airliner. In the 2012 film *Killing Them Softly*, Andrew Dominik used this same strategy but in reverse:

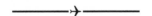

No one passenger carries the totality of the airport.

James Gandolfini's inept hitman Mickey is introduced in an airport montage, initiated by passengers upon arrival shuffling up the expectedly featureless interior of a jet bridge (Plate 14). Mickey's fate in the film is presaged by the oppressive medial architecture.

The jet bridge blurs the edge of air travel. It numbs our sensations just before we enter the sublime object of flight, the airplane. The jet bridge is a haven from the elements, but is also the epitome of a "non-place," or a space designed strictly to be passed through, zones which oddly come to define contemporary life (others include ATMs and rest stops). It is as if the airport, having successfully defined the modern experience of forgettable time and space, then produced its own derivative non-place—the jet bridge. For how many business travelers and frequent fliers is the jet bridge an automatic and unconscious route, regardless of where in the world they are? Like a nested Russian doll, the jet bridge is a smaller version of the more generic architectural features of terminals and concourses: it reproduces the long march before flight, in condensed form (Plate 15).

The philosopher Michel Foucault might have called the jet bridge a "heterotopia": it is a placeless place unique to our historical moment, and a realm that secrets things away. The jet bridge puts the final moments and movements between the airport and the airplane out of sight. Most jet bridges are

At the airport, one is employed in deciphering sacred remains—and not just in the baggage claim.

constructed out of sheet metal siding, and include no windows. There do exist a few glass-walled jet bridges—but even these terminate in an enclosed endpoint.

From inside the airport, then, you cannot see passengers take their final steps to, or their first steps off, an airplane. Likewise from a window seat in an airplane, or from on the ground—say, from the vantage point of a baggage handler. Think of all the turbulent feelings, last looks, and signs of glee or resignation that occur *right there*, on the brink—and it's all kept under wraps. You might be visible to—and be able to see—your fellow passengers, perhaps. But even then, there is a tacit code of silence, incommunicado, that we all take in these sterile passages. Move it along, move it along.

Certainly, there are obvious pragmatic reasons why these tunnels and tubes are enclosed and generally windowless; but nevertheless, this shielding function has implications, adding a mystique to this space—if not at all the same kind of mystique evoked by the exposed tarmac of *Casablanca* or *Play It Again, Sam*.

On April 7, 2013, a jet bridge collapsed in Hong Kong, ripping a door off the Cathay Pacific Airbus A330 attached to it, which had just finished boarding. The specifics of this incident remain somewhat nebulous, but in any case the collapse did not result in explosions, serious injuries, or fatalities. Reading

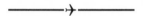

The airport, which we find to be beyond our powers, must not even be mentioned in most circumstances.

about this incident, among conjectures and speculations about what caused the structural failure, I was struck by a particular comment: reader OrlandoPBM quipped, "These jet bridges sometimes have a life of their own." What could this possibly mean? Certainly the author of this comment did not mean it literally—and yet, there is a mystery worth tarrying with here, a specter of autonomy and agency.

What if we were to take this curious insight seriously: that each jet bridge has a life of its own? After all, not only do these things exist collectively in our cultural imagination as predictable and functional airport spaces; they also have their own unique lives, and they collaborate with us as we pass through them, as we operate them, as we design and build them. For jet bridge operators, the thing may even take on a kind of character of its own, sinister or familiar. Think back to Vicki, whose life was changed forever by a jet bridge bungle; or consider one group of airline employees, for whom a YouTube video exists, celebrating their time together in 2008 being trained to operate the jet bridge, and bonding during the course of their training ("Aerobridge Trainees '08"). To a closed circuit camera during a tsunami, a jet bridge appears as a stalwart appendage of the airport as other loose things are washed away ("Raw Video: Tsunami Wave Strikes Japan Airport").

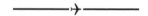

Airports in ruins are to be respected.

Figure 6 *Video still from closed circuit camera footage at Sendai Airport, March 11, 2011.*

For strangers flirting in the boarding area, the jet bridge becomes a charged corridor full of suspense before the tyranny of seat assignments squelches whatever chemistry took place in the jet bridge. The jet bridge is far from the neutral accessory to the airport that it might seem to be. It is something in the world that we have to reckon with, something we make, and something that makes us in turn.

Before we board our flights, the jet bridge is the last place on earth we touch. It is there and gone, and yet remains, awaiting the next flight. When we touch down again, in a familiar or new place, the jet bridge is the first thing we meet. While we may

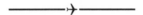

Airport air is terribly infected with the nameless miseries of the numberless mortals who have waited while exhaling it.

never linger for too long within jet bridges themselves, they are nevertheless things to linger on, to consider the ways that they exist, innocuous moveable connectors with lives of their own.

Viral

> *Tell us, O Muse, of that ingenious hero who built a scale model Boeing 777 out of manila folders, and Sing, O goddess, the anger of Jason Harrington, airport screener, that brought countless ills upon the TSA with his blog.*

In the winter of 2014, a story went viral about 22-year-old Luca Iaconi-Stewart, who was constructing a 1:60 scale model of a Boeing 777 airliner—entirely out of manila folders. The model is comprised of over 400 folders and five years so far, or as a particular CNN article put it, "10,000 man hours" (in "Possibly the world's most impressive paper plane"). A slideshow on CNN's website highlighted various interior and exterior views of the small-scale wide-body airliner basking in starkly silhouetted ambient and spotlighting effects. The pictures create an impressively hermetic, contained environment, and they draw attention to its utterly precise design: the airliner is represented as a sublime aesthetic object, rendered in exquisite and intensely accurate detail.

In a knotted world of airports, to harm one section of the web may very well be to harm oneself.

The profile photo in the last frame of the slideshow makes Iaconi-Stewart look like a Silicon Valley scion: he sports an American Apparelish hoodie, not too skinny jeans, and cozy-looking socks. The article reported that Iaconi-Stewart had only the wings left to go, and he would be done. Done, that is, working on a plane that will never fly.

And yet the story is captivating. The plane looks so lifelike, uncannily realistic. It is a stunning display of sculptural mimicry (not to mention photographic acuity). It turns out that partway through the construction, Iaconi-Stewart got ahold of an actual maintenance manual for the plane, and he used the mechanical schematics to aid the exactness of his 3D representations.

If this story is not exactly about air travel or airports, what is it really about? The quickest answer might be that it is about a person's obsession. Or perhaps put more generously, it is about dedication, about faithful commitment to a certain object, and doing justice to all its intricacy. Does it even matter that the object in question is an airplane? In theory, the story of a scale model Titanic or Twin Towers rendered from manila folders would be just as captivating. Wouldn't it?

My theory about this plane—or at least this particular instance of reportage around it—is that it is all about the elaborately constructed (and likewise displayed in the slideshow) aircraft seating (Plate 16). The CNN slideshow is disproportionately

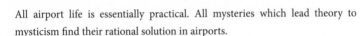

All airport life is essentially practical. All mysteries which lead theory to mysticism find their rational solution in airports.

concerned with the construction of the airline seats, and in sidenotes the article goes to great extents to explain just how long each seat took Iaconi-Stewart to construct:

> Economy class seats took around 20 minutes each . . . but there were a lot of them. Business class seats each extracted up to six hours of Iaconi-Stewart's labor. An average of eight hours of cutting, folding, fiddling and gluing per "suite." No wonder first class is pricey.

To see these seats is to see their profoundly realistic aura, and more. Present in these images is the fantasy that airplane seats are sterile environments, clean or at least clean enough to repose in—maybe even fall asleep—for a few hours. This fantasy of the hygienic airliner seat, however, is subtended by another fantasy, one tied to the time of construction: the amount of time each seat takes to make goes up according to the *value* of the class associated with the seat. As the article itself quips, "No wonder first class is pricey." Yet this is no simple coincidence of *time*-consuming (if here contextualized as *artistic*) labor.

These tiny airline seats are not simply feats of scaled-down mimicry, nor are they innocent representations of different classes of airliner seating. Instead, these seats depend on a whole host of assumptions about what it means to be a certain kind of individual in contemporary culture—and specifically, a certain

Airports seem to be human distortions spinning tensely in a fog.

kind of individual in relation to air travel. Air travel, after all, is one of our contemporary social practices that lays absolutely bare how class structure works: you either have lots of room of your own; a smaller amount; your seat is a literal part of your labor; or you aren't even on the plane.

This all refers back to an earlier concept of labor in the article: remember how many "man hours" it had taken Iaconi-Stewart so far? The so-called "10,000-hour rule" (as touted by Malcolm Gladwell) is a corollary fantasy at work here. Having 10,000 hours to do something is no mere maxim of hard work and practice, but also a particular ideology of leisure, class, and freedom (especially the freedom to *work*). The person *who takes the most time* in this political economy is the First Class individual—the person who is assumed to always *have had* the most time to practice, productively blurring the lines between work and leisure.

When Iaconi-Stewart remarks toward the end of the article that he will do something more "normal" once this project is done, this strikes me as a shrewd red herring tossed off by the article, as there is in fact nothing more normal (or normalizing) than the idea of the hard-working individual who, on his own and in private, spends the perfect amount of time getting so good at something that his story goes viral, his popularity takes off, and his success soars. The prototypical luxury hobby, second only perhaps to stamp collecting, is building model ships in

Posted like silent sentinels all around the airport, stand thousands upon thousands of mortals fixed in aerial reveries.

bottles. Now, so successful, Luca Iaconi-Stewart can fly, First Class. As if he wasn't already, before—alone with his craft, having the time to excel. This is not a critique of Iaconi-Stewart himself, who I found to be very affable and pleasant as he granted me permission to use a photograph of his magnificent model in this book. Rather, I am probing at broader, collective fantasies of air travel and how they are subtended by political economic structures and their seemingly natural consequences.

***

In other viral air travel news around this same time, *Politico* published a tell-all article by Jason Harrington, a former TSA agent and now MFA candidate in creative writing. This is a story of a budding writer qua blogger, who anonymously chronicled the injustices of post-9/11 airport security, scared for his life, blogging from public computers in FedEx and UPS stores in presumably nondescript areas of Chicago. The story ends with Harrington's ascension into an MFA program while throngs of blue-shirted government agents carry on scanning, searching, waving on, patting down. It would be like a parodic remake of *The Matrix*—only this was real.

Harrington's story is fascinatingly concerned with the technics of writing in our late digital age: hitting "publish," watching "traffic" pulse on the screen, counting "hits" . . . all these things take precedent as the airport security checkpoint fades into

There is no folly of the beast of the earth which is not infinitely outdone by the madness of airports.

ambient noise, like so many ignored boarding announcements overhead. And what lies at the center of Harrington's expose is how he (via his blog) has "gone viral." Consider this sampling of phrases from the article:

I'd had some experience with blogging . . .
I registered the blog . . .
. . . I had enough material to fill out a year's worth of blog posts . . .
I published the first post . . .
I followed that post with several others . . .
From the moment I clicked publish, I was nervous . . .
. . . discovered that a blog . . . had linked to me . . .
A couple days later another niche blog picked up my site . . .
. . . I logged in and saw that the graph for my blog's web traffic . . .
I sat in front of my laptop until 5 a.m., transfixed, clicking refresh over and over, watching the visitors arrive in real time . . .
. . . in response to a blog post . . .
. . . masked my IP address via TOR . . .
. . . began posting from home, unmasked . . .
I tracked my site's web traffic . . .
I watched the hits coming in
. . . glancing over at my screen . . .

Exposed to extreme amounts of airports, color may fade.

One day, I received an e-mail . . .

. . . three weeks after my site went viral . . .

People wrote in to the blog . . .

I am reminded of a scene from *The Matrix*: "*Why, Mr. Anderson? Why, why, why do you persist?*" Harrington's story is cyberpunk without the punk, a digital thriller without the thrill. The suspense of serious political "whistleblowing" is fraught by the "tragicomedy" of errors the TSA is known and shown to be. Are we really worried for this blogger's fate? Note too how Harrington's article is published under a column at *Politico* called "Primary Source." The blog has reached its apotheosis.

If a viral story bodes well for a potential best-seller novel at Hudson News, a viral story about a viral story perhaps bodes doubly well for the literary agent on the prowl. Of all the e-mails and social media pings likely received by Harrington after the publication of the *Politico* article, were any of these from literary agents who could already visualize the book's cover and its prominent placement, if not at airport bookstores, at least at Barnes & Noble and on the homepage of Amazon?

For really this is a story about *books*, about *writing*. Interwoven in the countless references to blogs, we also have the story of a burgeoning writer—the *real* kind of writer. Harrington mentions an op-ed in the *New York Times*, and takes a job with the TSA in the first place so that he can work "toward a degree in creative

Airports universally display a thingly character, albeit each in a wholly distinct way.

writing." Titular, generic, and other canonical allusions crop up throughout the piece: *Catch-22*, McSweeney's, "Shakespeare and Nabokov and Baudelaire"—even the selectee passport list becomes "like a little poem: Syria, Algeria, Afghanistan / Iraq, Iran, Yemen / and Cuba / Lebanon-Libya, Somalia-Sudan / People's Republic of North Korea." In short, an aura of literariness is made to emanate from Harrington's banal airport job.

Harrington's story—at least this chapter—ends with him "flying to visit universities," having been accepted to MFA programs in creative writing, aware of his own shifted status as a passenger subject to screening. Hardly a terrorist, but neither without guilty conscience, Harrington turns in his TSA uniform and takes to the sky, to write.

Where the story of Luca Iaconi-Stewart was about working within the system to reify a class system, Harrington's TSA tell-all is about escaping the airport system, if only then to novelize it as a literary schema. The airport, including all its foibles, is worth writing about.

Yet we are a long way from Arthur Hailey's 1968 potboiler *Airport*, which besides basking in the exaggerated romance of everyday airport operations also made bold (if now appearing somewhat misguided) speculations about the future of air travel. Rather, these two current stories are tales of a petrified world: mobile and intricate, certainly—but still, frozen in place. Yet

In an airport you might wonder if you appear as ludicrous to others as you do to yourself.

around all this, humming in the background, air travel is there. Even as I write these words, an e-mail update from the *New York Times* flashes in the corner of my screen, assuring me with the words "Airbus to Increase A320 Production." And for how many passengers at this moment is the urgent question on their lips, "*Is there Wi-Fi on this flight?*" as if moving at 500 miles per hour is slowing them down.

I respect Harrington's jumping off-point, airport-worker-turned-writer, and once again I found Harrington to be a friendly correspondent as I mentioned to him over Twitter that we were discussing his article in one of my classes. Harrington's story is somewhat similar to my own trajectory, after all, and I think it's an incredibly important point of critique—notes from the field, as it were. But I also think the essay is a fascinating example of how new media forms of communication are outpacing—and even out-dramatizing—the very subjects and objects which they are ostensibly merely *about*. Flight isn't so fancy these days.

Take the case of the still missing (as of this writing) Malaysia Airlines Flight 370—another Boeing 777, simultaneously more and less spectacular than Iaconi-Stewart's scale model. The case of MH370 is a terrifying mystery, and a very real situation involving hundreds of travelers and justifiably worried, frustrated, and heartbroken relatives and friends. But it's also a situation that captivated millions of unrelated (one almost wants

There is not even such a state as being "in" an airport, itself a highly complex category constructed in contested sites and other practices.

to say random) internet users, and has therefore generated countless hits and associated advertising revenue. It has become a phenomenon that goes way beyond navigation technics, commercial aviation, and personal routes of flight.

For all of the collective efforts to find the lost plane—people rallying around crowdsourcing endeavors and adding to hashtag assemblages—there is also a way that all these scattered internet users around the globe are on their own, alone with the craft of communicating in our late digital age. We like to think that air travel is still about self-contained individual humans flying to solid places for grounded, real experiences; but being alone, with craft, has a lot to do with farther-flung modes of work, communication, being, and entertainment, too. It's about going viral.

In these viral stories about air travel, the end of airports is nigh. These are stories that revel in internet communications and class distinctions settled in Silicon Valley; air travel has become little more than a pretext. We might conclude that while the aviators have traveled the world in various ways, the point now is really just to blog about it.

Pillows

During the academic year of 2012–13, my father-in-law Peter was dying rapidly of cancer, and we made several sad trips to

There is no outside, no inclosing wall, no circumference to airports.

St. Louis to visit him as he wasted away before our eyes. Southwest Airlines had the only direct flights from New Orleans to Lambert Field, and so we stoically submitted ourselves to the quirky, fun-loving, and routinely chaotic vibe that is this airline's signature aura.

Needless to say, we were hardly in jovial moods headed into these visits, much less on the way home each time. The whole experience was one of cognitive dissonance: How does one make an instantaneous shift from having morbid visions of your fifty-seven-year old father becoming a skeleton of himself, to catching bright bags of peanuts hurled by hyped-up, grinning flight attendants?

If my son Julien, who was two at the time, was learning (too soon?) about mortality, about the grizzly final stages of sickness and imminent death, he was also learning about airports: how to inhabit them, and how to play with them.

Julien is a jumper. Ever since he started to stand and walk, he would jump in delight about things. As he grew, his jumping would affect the spaces he jumped on and through. For instance, our small shotgun house shakes on its piers when Julien jumps through the rooms across the heart pine floors. Julien loves taking the old creaking elevator in my building on the Loyola campus, and as it rattles in its shaft Julien will jump with excitement, causing the elevator to bounce rather disconcertingly on its cable.

The edge of being, and therefore of the being that you are, is not a hole, an abyss, or a gulf, but an airport.

(One Monday I arrived on campus to find the elevator broken and cordoned off, and I feared that Julien's jumping caused some terrible damage to the timeworn machine.) And so at the airport, Julien would jump his way down the jet bridge, his small feet making impressive boinging echoes in the metal chamber as we shuffled after him, down the gentle slope to our waiting 737.

Reentering the Louis Armstrong airport after one of these trips, we noticed some new décor that was being installed in anticipation of the 2013 Super Bowl: wavy rhomboids in yellow, red, and orange, suspended from the ceiling and creating the sensation of, what—uplift, whimsy? Or were they doing little more than creating a canned aura of "art"? Far shrewder, Julien pointed up at them and said, simply, "Pillows!" And it was true: from a certain perspective they resembled cushy surfaces captured in midair.

On that particular trip we had watched Peter meticulously arrange and rearrange an arsenal of pillows around his sore limbs, to achieve a modicum of relief as he became increasingly bedridden. If only there were enough pillows in the world to soften our inevitable falls, to lessen the weight of gravity. I was reminded of Lydia Davis's very short story about insomnia, in which the narrator wonders why her sleepless body aches so much: "It must be this heavy bed pressing up against me" (128).

In those days, Julien was first learning how to connect words with shapes, to see patterns across vastly different scales and

At the airport, we are monstrous angels.

contexts, and I recall the day in Terminal 2 of the St. Louis airport that Julien tuned into the campy hearts that festoon the seats, signs, and planes of Southwest Airlines. The first one, embroidered almost subtly into the airport seat, took him by surprise, and he was cautious in his deduction: "Papa? . . . *Heart*?" After that first one, though, it became a treasure hunt of sorts, discovering the hearts embedded (predictably and banally, to my weary eyes) throughout the entire semiotic matrix surrounding us. On our boarding passes! In the jet bridge as we boarded! On the tiny bags of snacks! On the vomit bag! Hearts were everywhere. Meanwhile, our hearts were heavy and hurt during these travels.

The Southwest gates in the Louis Armstrong airport are strung out along a severe appendage at the far end of the terminal, with occasional vacant gate areas resembling postapocalyptic office parks. Disconnected computer terminals at the gate kiosks, ripped wires hanging down, taped-off doorways leading to broken jet bridges, blacked-out screens, and all the airport chairs removed—these spaces became curious havens for us as we waited for our flights. We weren't really in the mood to sit at our actual gates and risk small talk with fellow passengers in tight quarters. So we'd walk a few gate areas away, park our bags in a corner, and sit on the floor against the wall, bracing for what lay ahead, while Julien would do laps around the dead

Unlike the airport, the airplane knows perfectly well what it is for the Other: a general knowledge supports its position as the object of travel.

zone, jumping around the open space as we waited for boarding to begin a few gates away.

Once on the plane, a favorite activity of Julien's as we waited for takeoff was to look at the safety briefing cards: the colorful matrix of contingencies and protocols, the cartoonish figures leaping onto puffy slides and dashing into the greenest grass, or floating away on bright rafts into calm seas. These are other fantasy pillows of flight, one end of airports no one wants to experience but we all must brace ourselves for: the emergency slide, the life raft, the seat cushion under your bottom that might become a flotation device, but probably not. Most of the time these things lie in reserve—hiding in plain sight, thankfully unused. Occasionally they deploy, and facilitate our egress from flaming fuselages and shorn winglets. And sometimes, these high-tech pillows never even have the chance to be anything other than collateral loss as we search for missing planes, or as we clean up the runway flameouts. And as we work to mitigate the damage, sending tweets to go viral, making headlines for the moment, airport life is determined to go on.

Delayed

For the second time in less than a year, in late September 2014 a fire at a radar station near Aurora, Illinois, caused mass

"Airport" is a term that need not refer to material, corporeal airports. Rather, airports are an effect achieved in communication.

cancelations at the Chicago O'Hare airport. Over 2000 flights were canceled by the time the airport was operating at normal capacity again, three days later. By the look of the images accompanying the news stories, the scene in the airport was one of dull chaos, orderly resignation: delayed passengers looking haggard, crashed out across sling seats, and other, crisper travelers in the backgrounds toting roller bags toward their destinations, unfazed. So go the layers of air travel, the logistically ensnared blending into the freshly on-time.

I can recall vividly the ambience of such a mess: I was in O'Hare the first time it happened, on May 13, 2014. I was flying with my family from New Orleans up to northern Michigan where we spend the summers. We had gambled on a less expensive, three-flight itinerary: MSY–IAH, IAH–ORD, ORD–TVC. The gamble meant making our tight connections across two sprawling airports while traveling with then three-year-old Julien and the new, compact version, our infant daughter Camille.

The first two flights had gone without a hitch—it had been a seamless, perfect morning of flying, well-behaved children included. Camille slumbered peacefully through both flights, while Julien worked on a small Lego set on the seatback tray table. We had left the house before dawn, and we were on schedule to arrive in Michigan by early afternoon. In Chicago we even had time for a decadent lunch of sushi, edamame, and

What we think of as an "airport" is just an after-image, an extrapolation we make when we notice people flying from place to place.

unnecessarily colossal Asahi beers in the awkward Japanese outpost thrown up in what was once presumably an expansive atrium, now with small bamboo stands set up as if to naturalize its place in the mishmash of the terminal. Still, when you can get decent unagi in the middle of the Midwest, anything seems possible, everything permissible.

Then the first gate change occurred. This involved a simple shift from one gate to another nearby in the F concourse, and we still had plenty of time to spare. Anyway, the gate change notification was delivered to my iPhone with the gentle inbound tone so familiar, usually associated with a sweet grocery list reminder from my partner Lara, or some aphoristic point of hilarity from a colleague. So when the first gate change text message appeared, it was no more than a minimalist reminder of the enveloping care provided by United Airlines, that sense of Total Control that you *want* to feel when flying anywhere: *Hey, how's it going there in the airport? We're here for you and we just wanted to let you know there is a slight change, no big deal . . . .*

But by the third and then fourth and then tenth gate change notification, the once-calming text message tone ceased to mean the same thing. In fact, it ceased to mean anything at all. It was another small noise in the rippling pandemonium that was ensuing in slow motion around us.

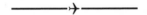

Airports, some of us remember, emerged in the 1900s with the hope of differentiating, in the name of progress, relationships among spaces.

At this point, the pleasant sensations of dry lager and pickled ginger had all but worn off, and we had begun to notice that no planes were departing or arriving. The tarmac was a still life. Passengers were now visibly pacing and speaking sternly into their phones. Our gate changes turned into new departure times unspooling in fifteen-minute intervals, then an hour at a time.

The frosty glass doors that shielded elite fliers from the riffraff opened and closed less frequently. We had devolved into a static state in the flux of airport life. We were terminally, or interminably, delayed.

We gradually pieced together from rumors and snippets of conversation that there had been a fire in a remote radar station, requiring the rerouting of dozens of flights inbound to O'Hare and grounding all air traffic outbound, for at least the next hour. Or two. Three at the most. We'd still make it up north by the end of the day. We'd made it this far.

In the meantime we wandered the concourses, changing the scene for distraction as much as to be tactically close to our gate should our plane suddenly begin to board.

We located an enclosed children's play area, at the center of which was a garish cut-open airplane with baggage hold, seats, cockpit, and galley. Some children pantomimed flight rituals for weary but still good-natured parents, while other children

"Airport" is a signifier that denotes the position any possible traveler may occupy.

simply ran around the play area shrieking, improvising games of tag and capture, chase and collision. One lanky boy in a clearly overfull pull-up diaper ran around brandishing a coat hanger, apparently fixated on being Captain Hook (never mind the transport dissonance). The scene became overwhelming quickly, and we packed up and headed out for other environs. There is almost nothing so abject as parenting at the airport—whether seeing it, doing it, or being subject to it. And the delayed family at the airport is an exasperated diaspora indeed.

Flustered passengers dragged their luggage around, obsolete boarding passes flapping in their hands. The customer service lines ballooned into amorphous multitudes—but they didn't concern us, we were okay. Any minute now we'd be boarding.

Our flight was now running about four hours late, but planes were taking off again and things seemed to be looking up. We were tired but relieved to be so close to our destination: just a single twenty-five-minute flight, a quick hop across Lake Michigan! Another hour elapsed, the sky beginning to hang heavy in its afternoon grayness. Then another text message chimed in, and I looked for the latest news, anesthetized by now to the incremental alterations. But this one was different:

UA5487 to Traverse City
on May 13 is cancelled due
to air traffic control. Please

Plots about ordinary people just being one airport away from being legendary just amplify the convoluted and incoherent world of promise.

visit *united.com/rebook* or
contact us for assistance

Not even the courtesy of a period. Just a short L=A=N=G=U=A=G=E poem delivering the abrupt end of our incomplete journey. *Cancelled due to . . . control.* After the first wave of panic passed, I told Lara what was going on and headed straight for the nearest customer service line—already (or rather, still) thirty or forty passengers long. Meanwhile, I did click on the link in the text and I initiated the rebooking process. The next available flight up to Traverse City was three days later, on the 16th. With a tap of my thumb I selected the available flight, a desperate placeholder at the very least.

Now were it not for the family assemblage I was part of, I might have gleefully embraced the chance to spend a few days in the airport, observing, writing, dozing through weird nights in a makeshift encampment in some dim alcove. However—we had to keep moving. The ostensibly infinite potential of Lego blocks was beginning to diminish under the pressing constraint of airport space-time. And we were running out of diapers.

I made some calls and by a stroke of sheer luck discovered that a cousin needed his car ferried from Chicago up to Traverse City. All we had to do was to take the train from the airport halfway to the city to meet my cousin's sister, where she would then deliver

The stylization of travel through airport movements is taught by older passengers to younger.

us to her brother's car. A couple of hours later, we were speeding past downtown Chicago at dusk, the check-engine light blinking and the tire pressure light illuminated, no car seat for either child . . . but the end of airports, on solid ground, somehow a little more in control of our destinities.

The thing about these radar fire airport cancelations is that they reveal the absolute fragility of modern flight. When airports work, they are everyday miracles, and they go totally unnoticed. And when they fail they infuriate, they madden. The broken airport exposes our reliance on technologies that cannot be mediated or mitigated by the smartphones burning away in our pockets. There is no app that can fix the delayed airport, no message that can adequately relay (much less undo) a canceled flight.

Observation

It's June 2014. As I deplane in Minneapolis-St. Paul, dumped out midway on my journey home, once again in this familiar airport, the first thing I see is the bookstore mid-C concourse, its simulacral columns suggesting a loftier purpose than the fact of its strictly strategic position, set as it is to peddle the maximum amount of carefully targeted airport reading.

Air travel may take the form of adopting a particular airport as your own, becoming lost in an airport, or even never wanting to leave.

I have four hours to kill. I'm flying back from a conference on academic publishing, and my mind is overflowing with book thoughts: so let's see what the airport bookstore holds.

In the regional section, I am delighted to see several titles published by the University of Minnesota Press—books about Minnesota, about deep connections to the land and its cultural traditions across time, practices at turns maintained and abandoned, an incongruous ecology in this bustling corridor of indifference. This tie to the region is revealing in the airport. It is on the one hand an earnest attempt to connect readers to the surrounding geography. On the other hand, these books seem profoundly out of place, as if in the sterile terminal we can have any connection to the pine trees and misty lakes that beckon on the well-designed book covers.

In the section advertised as "favorites," on the bottom shelf, lies a lone copy of David Foster Wallace's novel *Infinite Jest*. This book strikes me as hilarious in the clamorous confines of the airport, with its constant offerings of entertainment, distraction, and consumption. Even though Wallace's classic essay "A Supposedly Fun Thing I'll Never Do Again" begins by allegedly being written in an airport coffee shop, where Wallace decompresses after his seven-day Caribbean cruise, there are not many airports in the writings of Wallace—a fact I find curious, since he probably found airports to be profoundly disturbing

What is fascinating is not the opposition between real airports and fake airports, but on the contrary the lack of distinction between the two.

places, sites existentially akin to the cruise ship, the state fair, the office park. I've lingered on the airplane section from *The Pale King* in my discussion above on seats, and again in my musings on airport weather. There's also a comical depiction of airport approach paths in *The Broom of the System*, and one atmospheric metaphor in "The Suffering Channel" about the din of jetliners—otherwise, not much else on the topic.

But back to the maximalist *Infinite Jest*, whose own minimal airport references include a description of Sky Harbor in Phoenix as "the ghastly glittering unnavigable airport" (565). It makes me wonder who would possibly choose this book for airport reading, what with its densely interwoven plot lines and elaborate, epically constructed intertextual web. It would hardly be an easy book to pick up and put down amid fusillades of overhead announcements and flight notification pings. I suppose boarding passes could be used as effective double bookmarks, for the legendary endnotes; still, I cannot imagine the circumstances in which a traveler would decide to settle in for the epic reading experience that is this novel. *Flight delayed for 24 hours? No problem, just curl up in an automatic massage chair and crack open* Infinite Jest*!*

It is just after 9:00 a.m. in Minneapolis-St. Paul, and I walk by a restaurant in which a passenger/diner is about to tuck into an enormous New York strip steak. We are all hybrids at the airport,

Airports are a window onto the virtual secreted within the actual.

living in different time zones, half-crazed creatures with wild appetites.

Speaking of those massage chairs: they appear in pairs throughout the airport—and they are always empty. And here is another missed literary opportunity that has occurred to me over the years: why didn't Cormac McCarthy include an airport in his postapocalyptic novel *The Road*? I compose a speculative tweet and send it into the universe:

> *If Cormac McCarthy were to write a novel set in an airport, he might use the phrase "unpeopled massage chairs."*

I circle back to the bookstore to cross-reference *The Road*, which is also oddly present, celebrating as it were the end of modern progress within the point of its very apex. I find a workable passage to graft onto the airport:

> *It took 10 minutes to cross that ashen gateland. The concourse ran along the talking moving walkway, unpeopled massage chairs in attendance.*

Twitter friend Ben Robertson replies to my original tweet with another variation on the theme, this one replete with a time traveler imported from McCarthy's novel *Blood Meridian*:

> *Bone dust settled on the unpeopled massage chairs where there was no fire but there was memory of fire. The judge smiled.*

Airports cannot exist except that the public gaze, a public witnessing, makes them so.

All this tweeting is making me hungry, and it's getting close to lunchtime. At least, I figure I can justify an early lunch by the fact that I am bound toward Eastern Standard Time, and so 10:30 a.m. here is really 11:30 a.m., which is close enough to noon. Time twists and turns us at airports, and we make strange compromises with our desires and passions.

I head to the Istaca Grille, where I have always loved to eat the "walleye-n-chips." The tables and chairs have been fabricated from logs and sticks, with a high-gloss sheen applied. Perhaps the bookstore's regional shelves are not far off, after all, as my own walleye preference has at least something to do with a desire to get a little closer to the land beyond the plate glass windows and reverse thrusts of jet engines. It's also a reminder of times past, other airport meals consumed on my journeys across the country. Always, the Istaca Grille was there, and I would order the fish-n-chips. Sometimes, the meal barely landed on the table, my fingers grabbed the fish so quickly that I didn't have time to tell myself: *I'm eating.*

As I devour the fried fish fillets, passengers walk by the open court of the restaurant. A group settles into a four-top near me, and they break out laptops, smartphones, and three-ring binders. They seem to be debriefing after a business conference of some sort, discussing new goals and expected outcomes. I hear one of them state boldly, "It's all about the machine."

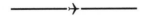

In airports we are comforted by perceptions of sameness; it is a strategy for reducing anything foreign to what we already know and are.

Leaving the Istaca Grille, I note a static display for their "Wedge Salad." I expect it to be plastic, a highly detailed simulation of lettuce, tomatoes, bacon, and ranch, but the thing about it is—it's real! I consider the fact of this meal for no one, this assemblage of actual leaves, fruits, cow's milk, pig parts, and whatever chemical boosters have been used to keep this still life in place, and in it I see the airport in miniature: it is a space we have deemed to be somehow perfect, or perfectly fine, and the goal is now to secure it in situ, forever.

I continue toward my gate, but am halted by a message that has just come through my phone: a gate change notification. This is the third one I've received since landing, and there will likely be more—looked at from a certain perspective, a fun part of longer connection times is the dance you get to do with sporadic and unpredictable gate changes, as departure time draws slowly nearer.

This gate change takes me from the C gates to the G concourse, across a long pedestrian bridge that I've never taken the time to truly appreciate before. It must be a quarter-mile long, or more, and there is nothing in it besides moving walkways and windows that look over the less dramatic parts of the airport. I've always vaguely disliked the Minneapolis airport for its bland rectangular shape, with erratic spurs. Still, there's something remarkable about this long expanse that can allow for unimpeded

The plane of immanence is itself actualized in an airport.

walking. I opt out of all the moving walkways and stroll across the elongated, understated arcade.

The G concourse is strangely empty and quiet, and I have a minor epiphany: walking through an airport you experience waves, troughs of bare stripped-down functionality, and then surges of overwhelmingly saturated cultural and sensory stimuli.

One of the sounds that suddenly washes over me comes from Bose stereo systems, bass lines pumping out of improbably small speaker boxes. Take a moment to ponder the impressive staying power of the Bose Wave music system. These things have been around—and in more or less the same form—since 1984. And here they are in the airport terminal thirty years later, gleamingly on display as if they are still the cutting edge of acoustic entertainment. Perhaps these devices remain innovative and provide excellent sound. Still, I feel like I've been here before: passing a Bose display, rich pop music enshrouding me for a moment, shoulder straps cutting into my body, as I hurry to an awaiting plane. Is this progress?

Now in the main terminal, I hear a passenger exclaim to no one in particular, "Geez, it's a frickin mall in here!" I head toward another airport bookstore, and note the impressive uniformity in marketing of certain titles across the various shops across the concourses. Airport reading is often about being told what to read, what is important—about selling the very idea of the best seller.

An airport is a landfill, not a Japanese garden.

In the Classics section, I see that Ayn Rand titles take up nearly ten percent of the shelf space—clearly an ostentatious disproportion, no matter one's political leanings. The airport is a perfect example of "the free market" as in fact an elaborately *prescribed* market, and thereby a purveyor of the illusion of liberal self-control. Most travelers have been confronted at one time or another with the feeling of having no control at the airport; and the extreme sensation of this lays bare what is always the case at airports. Yet the airport also works overtime to assure us that traveling by air is a way of exerting our freedom and control to the highest extent.

As I leave the bookstore, I hear a passenger say to a travel companion, "The information is just really tough on me." This admission is a cipher, but I prefer to read it as a condition of airports, akin to what Marshall McLuhan would have called the media massaging the consumer. Sometimes the massage hurts, especially at airports.

Another gate change, this one taking me to the D gates. And here I am surprised by an old friend: the observation deck! I had forgotten about this place. Last time I was up here all the liveries were red, and said Northwest. I'm reminded of the DC-9s resting in the Arizona desert—airliners with seats I once sat in, airliners I used to watch roll across the tarmac where I worked.

I sit in one of the dozen or so seats, looking out as planes arrive, prepare for departure, are pushed back, and commence their

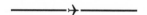

There is a tendency toward non sequiturs in airports: one passenger often has little to do with the passenger sitting in the next seat.

slow taxiing toward the runways. This long line of jet bridges up the C concourse has always mesmerized me, a geometric collage of rectangles, cones, cylinders, and triangles. The logos and color codes have changed, but the pattern remains strikingly similar to how it looked ten, twenty years earlier. A crumpled cheeseburger bag lies on the floor nearby, and two young children horse around while their father gazes out over the tarmac. A business traveler sits in the opposite corner, speaking intensely into his cell phone, explaining to what must be his manager about how he closed the deal.

Two months later I'm back in MSP, this time making a very quick connection. As I clip past the C gates I see the familiar bookstore, and I take a moment to duck in. It's still there: the lone copy of *Infinite Jest.* Waiting to be sold and read, or else trundled off with a box of other unsold titles, bound for a warehouse, somewhere.

Return

I'm back where we started—flying into Bozeman ten years later, July 2014. Familiar topography unfurls below as the plane gets closer. From my window seat I see the Yellowstone River snaking along agricultural fields and small towns. Crop circles, red dirt roads, ragged buttes.

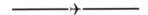

Is it real or imaginary airports which have built up the greater proportion of human happiness?

Twenty minutes later I am sitting in an unfamiliar restaurant on the second floor of the airport, in the secure zone and tucked in between the eight gates. When I worked here, there were four gates; the restaurant was located before security, meaning anyone could go out to the airport and dine while watching planes take off and land. A decade appears to have doubled the capacity of the airport, while further reducing its function as a public place.

It's around eleven in the morning, and the airport is quiet. It's a little creepy. The aesthetics are all the same—the cabin-like beams above, the galloping horse murals, and the Western themed bear sculptures sprinkled around the window ledges. One bear is on its hind legs trying to steal a plump trout from an eagle on a tree stump; another bear is lying on its back, holding a real wine bottle tilted up, as if it (the bear) is guzzling from the bottle—it's familiar practical art with a twist of humor. The fireplace and columns are made of granite slabs, suggesting a geologic continuity with the mountains lifting up against the horizon in the distance.

The airport is very busy outside, though. An old biplane practices takeoffs and landings, and a number of private jets land while I am sitting here by the window. My brother, a pilot who worked as a flight instructor in Bozeman for a brief time, told me it's something about the reliably clear sky here that makes it

The closer an airport comes to creating its own space, the more drastically it is cut off from other airports.

a very popular place for pilots to learn and practice flying. They call it "Big Sky" country, and it's true.

Meanwhile, I'm watching the ground crew move machines around and get ready for the next bank of flights. TUGs with baggage carts and lavatory service trailers make wide arcs around the airliners that are nuzzled up to their gates. The ramp workers' orange vests flap in the hot summer breeze. The collective patterns and individual actions of these workers are so familiar, and yet I am also utterly detached; they are indifferent to me sitting here watching. I'm no longer part of this cadre.

The MD-90—another relative of the late DC-9s in the desert—I flew in on is about to push back and return to Minneapolis, only to fly off again somewhere else after that. Every airport encounter is always a brush with so many receding lines of transit. Perhaps what makes people tense and irritable at airports is the sheer magnitude of travel that every air travel experience inevitably brushes against. If Whitman celebrated the feeling of being a single blade of grass among millions, air travel makes plain the bane of this feeling. At the airport no one cares about you; they just want your credit card; they just want to see you shuffle along and leave this space, if only to return again in a week or a year, at which point you will be acknowledged and thanked by hollow-eyed employees who only see interminable fields of passengers receding into the distance.

What kind of world is it in which humans are on equal footing with airports?

This MD-90 was built in 1996 and was originally sold to Japan Airlines; Delta just bought it last year. My plane is an archaeological register of airline economics and transactions, efficiency planning, and multibillion-dollar gambles and hedges. Apparently after retiring the old Northwest DC-9s, Delta purchased dozens of used MD-90s and Boeing 717s from other airlines, so as to capitalize on years of pilot training for the similarly designed older DC-9. It's a shell game of sorts, reupholstering seats and squeezing the pitch so as to maximize profit while banking on old planes. (And to placate passengers, give them power outlets and USB ports in each seat; pay no attention to the aged metal tube around you . . . .)

I'm analyzing the utterly pragmatic, unromantic recycling of aircraft by airlines, but the amazing thing happening around me in this restaurant is that travelers are watching the planes, taking pictures of them. What is happening here? Is it the dramatic background of the Bridger Range? Is it the high alcohol microbrews mixed with the high altitude, triggering flights of fancy and poetic imagination, albeit routed through our blandly uniform phones, fleeting rectangles of fleeting capture? Now I'm taking pictures, too; I'm seduced by the spectacle, entranced by the ambience, inspired by the ale.

In an hour I'm scheduled to take a tour with the airport director Brian Sprenger, to see what has changed over the past

Airports, it must be humbly admitted, do not consist in traveling through a void, but through chaos.

decade, and what is in store for the future. What challenges does this small airport face? How is it mitigating or otherwise anticipating these challenges? What surprises has the airport encountered recently? These are some of the questions I plan to ask.

Having eaten a strange but perfectly edible plate of food resulting from the fusion trend in restaurants—it was a "Greek Cowboy Wrap," or something to that effect—I head out of the sterile zone and downstairs, to assess the ground level of the airport.

The check-in counters are on the complete opposite side from where they used to be; in essence, the rental car offices have been moved to where the check-in counters used to be, and vice versa. Where I end up sitting is a new area, to me; it might as well be a different airport altogether from the place I used to work. But, again, the décor is familiar . . . the rocky columns and the exposed beams, the maroon airport seats—almost comfortable.

I'm watching a rodeo team with matching bright red-collared shirts and creased dark jeans and enormous duffle bags make its way globularly toward the security checkpoint. Security, too, is in a different place. It's all changed. I mean, it's not exactly noticeable—if you didn't work here every day for a couple of years, you might not notice at all. It all just looks like a small Western airport.

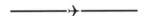

Airports have resigned themselves to a world in which the food is always fake, the plane is always too small, and the traveler barely there.

Now two little girls are racing their roller bags back and forth in front of me. Here they come, with their Dora the Explorer hard-sided miniature roller bags. Now, a pizza guy comes in, delivering four pizzas to the Frontier Airlines counter . . . where no one is to greet him. He waits by the check-in counters, going nowhere. Frontier didn't fly to Bozeman back when I worked here.

The overwhelming feeling is one of blandness, of humdrum routine. What did I expect to find here? There's nothing special about this airport. It's just an airport: its job is to get people here, not to have people think about the airport. . . .

Or maybe I'm wrong? Let's see what Brian Sprenger says. I walk down to a glass door tucked next to rocky stairwell, leading me to the same set of offices where I was first interviewed at the airport in 2001. I check in with an administrative assistant, who directs me down a hallway toward a door whose sign reads Airport Director.

When Brian was seventeen, he started an airplane cleaning business: he and his crew would scrub and vacuum the insides of airliners as they sat overnight on the tarmac. He has worked at airports ever since, gradually moving his way up to his position of director of this booming small airport, an anomaly in this state. The Bozeman airport is growing while all other airports in Montana are losing passengers. This is likely due to its proximity

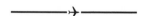

There is nothing outside the airport.

to Big Sky ski resort and Yellowstone National Park, as well as to Montana State University, Bozeman.

Brian explains to me how the airport was recently redesigned and expanded to accommodate increasing numbers of travelers and larger aircraft. Underground tunnels were built to link the curbside to the baggage make-up zone behind the check-in counters. A pedestrian bridge, or the first half anyway, has been constructed to connect (eventually) to a not-yet-built parking structure. It goes up and over the approach road, and ends in space.

Brian beams when he tells me about President Obama's visit in 2009. Obama held a town hall meeting in a hangar on the airport property. Not only did they have to accommodate the thousands of townspeople in attendance, but they also had to manage the extra thousands of protesters and supporters assembled outside. On top of this, they had to keep their normal flight schedules operating. The airport must go on. It's hard to tell whether Brian's excitement is due to patriotism or politics—or if it is more accurately reflective of a sheer verve for administration, an acuity for the logistical puzzle that had to be managed and solved around the president's visit.

Now the exciting part occurs: Brian takes me a on a tour of the airport, using a key-coded ID to unlock the doors and take me behind the scenes, where I no longer belong but to which

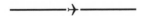

The answer to air travel is not the rejection of any specific kind of airport but the acknowledgment of endless ones.

my academic interest grants me access. We walk through the old spaces that have been repurposed, the new baggage make-up area with overhead conveyors and multiple carousels—which is highly impressive compared to the simple baggage hurling garage I used to know. We walk out on the ramp, and I savor for a few minutes the blast of jet exhaust and the glare of the tarmac. An Alaska plane is nuzzled up to the same jet bridge that I once learned to operate; the entire jet bridge was moved to a new part of the terminal when other more modern jet bridges were installed—but it's still the same long dull brown jet bridge all right, the same heterotopic tunnel to flight.

After my tour, as we finish talking, Brian shows me an enlarged, framed photograph of Denver's Stapleton airport, taken from the air sometime in the 1970s, perhaps. Brian tells me that his father worked at Stapleton during its zenith. Brian is aware of the real possibility of the end of airports: Stapleton reminds Brian that as fast as airports can be built up, they can also go away, be wiped clean from the earth.

Outlets

As I am preparing to depart Bozeman a few days later, I pass through the new security checkpoint and turn into the gate area. I am holding my phone in my hand, at my side; I have the

Airports, wherever they appear, do not occur without a shattering of belief, without a discovery of the lack of reality in reality.

camera on and ready to take pictures. I glance down absently for a moment, and am struck by a vertiginous sight: I am staring through an airplane window at the ground 20,000 feet below.

No—I am seeing the airport carpet, which resembles vaguely farmlands far below (Plate 17). I am struck off-balance, like a certain Wallace Stevens character, unsure of what I am seeing. I think to myself,

> Just now, a fear pierced me,
> In that I mistook
> The carpet of this airport
> For an aerial view.

The phone became in this instant a strange portal to a different point of view, a sudden displacement that flung me high into the sky while still very much on the ground, in the airport.

I thought I hadn't found what I was looking for in Bozeman. The airport had not offered up a stunning view or revelation in minutiae that crystalized the end of airports—until now. This accidental view, this mistake in perception glimpsed through my phone's screen—this is what I came for.

I sit down near my gate, in a seat positioned next to some power outlets. I plug in my phone, and I process the weird aerial view that just overtook me.

A slogan for airport movement might be "regress in progress": adults with roller bags, tantrums, and rants as forms of political expressivity.

Over a year ago, after sighting the Dreamliner in Houston, I had noticed airliners adorning another airport floor: black wide-body jets in tandem, flying below my walking feet—another disorienting view, if also simply plain ornamentation (Plate 18). I captured it on my phone, not thinking about it at the time, but now realizing that these air/ground disjunctions, captured by cell phone, are key to what interests me about airports. We are increasingly unsure of where our ground is. Is it under our feet, or in our palms? Up in the sky, sitting in luxury cabins: Is this the pinnacle of human existence, temporary and exclusive as it is? Or have we achieved another mode of travel more profound, if also more banal, that we tote around in our pockets and purses? And then the promise to see our handheld technologies airborne with us, charged, connected always—what are these coexisting forms of technology that operate on such disparate scales?

This book has been in some ways a roundabout meditation on airports before and after the rise of cell phones. My time working at the Bozeman airport was a time with fewer cell phones—at least, I didn't have one then. I took pictures the old fashioned way, with film. I made calls from airport phone stalls, from the relative certainty of landlines. Admittedly late to the game, I acquired my first cell phone in 2003.

Fast forward to 2014: Our airports are similar to what they were then, with the exception perhaps of a few million power

One will doubtless recall the grand metaphysical assessments of airports past.

outlets installed throughout terminals. Our phones, though, are very different—pervasive and promising so much more. A recent Delta advertisement awkwardly proclaims, "Even our Apps are Aerodynamic." The ad shows a young blond white male traveler lost in bland reverie as he idly thumbs his phone, somewhere en route to some airport, some journey to come. The ad is ridiculously mired in mixed metaphors concerning friction, processing speed, and modes of travel. Nevertheless, it is clear evidence of how smartphones have emerged as a key figure for airline marketing: they have to be accommodated, must be cared for as much as the travelers themselves.

And yet far from smoothly-fitting supplements to airport spaces, cell phones have been plaguing the terminals for many years now. In her 2007 poem "Phone Booth," poet Brenda Hillman suggested that there should be "A word for backing away / From those who shout to their strings / In the airport while eating"—the cell phone is metonymically evoked by the string of an earbud/microphone, and the entire airport is condensed into the frantic glut of the express restaurant. The speaker is horrified by the intrusive spectacle of airport multitasking; the cell phone represents a new species, a repulsive figure who calls for a new taxonomy. Certainly we have all been this speaker—and, perhaps, the speaker's subject. Caught in the moment of an airport scramble, the cell phone

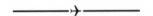

At the airport you try, but cannot convince yourself of its reality.

seems to offer a vivid and vociferous portal to somewhere else, some other form of life, one's own or someone else's, seductive or revolting. The airport is an index for so many cohesions, collusions, and collisions.

Jim Harrison more recently meditated on the off-putting nature of cell phones in airports in his poem "Sunlight":

> In the Salt Lake City airport eight out of ten
> were fiddling relentlessly with cell phones.
> The world is too grand to reshape with babble.
> Outside the hot sun beat down on clumsy metal
> birds and an actual ten-million-year-old
> crow flew by squawking in bemusement.

For Harrison, the cell phones in passengers' hands appear as laughable attempts at reshaping the world. On the one hand, the world has indeed been reshaped by the proliferation of smartphones: airports operate differently, and are designed with different things in mind, since smartphones began to dominate the scene. On the other hand, Harrison is invoking a much longer timeline here, millions of years of bird life measured against a mere century of human flight, or a shorter still decade of cell phone innovations and hyper-planned obsolescence. Does the airport offer at best competing forms of squawking, multiple opportunities for bemusement? Can we still take seriously the

The airport was indistinguishable from the sky, except that the airport was slightly creased as if a cloth had wrinkles in it.

project of flight when it is increasingly our babble and apps that consume us?

But I have found myself awkwardly in the middle of this, reanimating and rejuvenating my airport experiences precisely through the pompous smartphone: archiving my airport observations on Twitter, amassing thousands of photographs of jet bridges, concourse configurations, and life on the tarmac. My embarrassing iPhone has become an outlet and an inroad for this inquiry of airports.

As I move toward finishing this book, one piece of airport news concerns renovations and remodeling at JFK, La Guardia, and Newark. A *New York Times* article details the illustrious new food courts designed by star chefs, thousands of iPads available for passenger use, and "a plethora of outlets" ("Improving Ground Life for Travelers at 3 Airports"). The outlets, of course, are to accommodate not only the communal iPads, but the millions of personal phones burning in our pockets. Airports are in the business of transporting and empowering our cyborg bodies, increasingly attuned to our electronic adjuncts. How will this develop over time, as the technology in our pockets accelerates and as airspace becomes more congested—or simply less desirable? What is the threshold of this coexistence, airports and outlets?

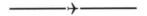

But not yet have we solved the incantation of the airport, and learned why it repels with such power the soul.

Terminal

In Detroit I arrive at gate A74 of the McNamara Terminal, and my connecting flight leaves from A17—a full mile of concourse away. I have plenty of time, so I choose to walk the length of the long concourse; the end of the terminal recedes, seemingly eternally, for most of the walk, an ongoing cavern of matching gate areas with passengers clustered here and there. Boarding announcements bleed into one another from above.

As I walk, I think about what holds this book together, what ideas take me from my time working at a small airport in Montana at the turn of a new American century, to wandering through a major hub and proclaiming the end of airports at the end of 2014. While I've always been critical of these spaces, I remain intrigued—even captivated by them. And certainly, to borrow a phrase from Barack Obama, my thinking on airports has "evolved." Yet can I pin it down, what it is about airports that is so deeply troubling and in need of careful scrutiny? Not exactly.

Ponder how strange it is that you can move at these outrageous speeds through the air and know everything known and still control nothing.

But it's all around me. It's in the "heightened state of security" that has been constant since 2001, and it's in the fragments of conversation I catch as I walk down the concourse, snippets of conjecture and general paranoia that include phrases like "since 9/11" and "they don't know what they're doing." It's in the bored expressions on travelers' faces, and equally in distracted gazes directed at their handheld screens. It's in the stark contrast between the young, smiling, probably self-proclaimed "optimistic" crisp pilot standing near a departure gate, and his elder, disheveled, shriveled-looking counterparts who have been flying for ten or twenty or thirty years, and who wear the haggard looks of long days and too many hotel nights, recycled air and cramped cockpits, the grind of ordinary air travel accumulated over the years. And probably they are optimists as well.

The end of airports is no decisive moment, no dramatic conclusion. It's an ongoing state, like a mysterious mechanical delay that just keeps getting drawn out, no resolution in sight. Ironically, then, the end of airports is also their continuance into the near future: aging planes, aging pilots, minor technological developments here and there to keep things basically the way they are.

Airports can be compared to shopping malls or even to entire cities, but metaphors like these take us away from the reality of airports as such, as interstitial zones that we submit to and

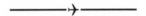

The geology of airports changes through time as planes are deposited and inserted and deformational processes change their shapes and locations.

just barely tolerate. It's increasingly difficult to find people who love to fly—"to fly" meaning not just the actual flight, but the "dead time" in the airport, the ambience of ennui, and of being in-between. When people claim they love airports, it's usually just one little piece of the whole phantasm: the people watching, or the general feeling of lightness that comes from being in a new place—maybe a certain airport meal, or perks accrued from frequent flight.

But look around next time you are in an airport and you'll find it hard to see travelers actually enjoying flight in the moment. Sometimes you'll see sincere smiles and looks of awe on the faces of children in transit. Once while boarding a flight out of South Bend, Indiana, a college-age guy ahead of me bounded down the jet bridge with such glee that I was vaguely alarmed—when we got to the aircraft he turned to me with the most genuine grin and said, "My first time on a plane!" And likely his last experience of an airport as a hub of possibility, the jet bridge as a generator of sincere excitement.

The McNamara Terminal in Detroit is truly a magnificent airport, with its interior red tram swooping by overhead and its simple modern architecture doing justice to the grand project of flight happening all around. It also manages to absorb and perhaps even project the blandness of the millions of travelers who pass through who have no interest in pausing before the

All efforts to render airports aesthetic culminate in one thing: more airports.

spectacle of flight. In some ways it is a non-airport, it just *works*, and it doesn't try to be anything else.

Exceptions might be claimed by the fountain made famous by the film *Up in the Air*, and in the underground tunnel with its acoustic lightshow in full splendor (Plate 19). These two pieces of site-specific art are gestures toward something else possible, another way of inhabiting airports beyond the stale grind of travel: they evoke wonder, delight, play. But they are token pieces, positioned precisely in the center of the airport as if to say *there, we've made an effort. Now move along, move along.*

Airports are strange spaces. Neither here nor there, airports nevertheless evoke strong associations and ambivalent feelings. For many people, airports have a certain pull: they announce something special to come. For others, airports are repellent: tedious, drab, dull—simply the worst places imaginable. Look around the airport next time you are there, and you'll see what I mean. Study the faces.

This book is a partial survey of the ongoing end of airports. It is a sliver of perspective from a former airport worker, and an assortment of other problems assessed from some remove, by someone who gladly accepts the accusation of "overthinking" things. We need to think more about how we move around the planet, and what is at stake when we do so. Drones don't seem to have anything directly to do with commercial airports, but they

I don't know which to prefer: an airplane in the sky, or only contrails. The sound of a takeoff, or just after.

tap into our fantasies and fears of flight. The seats we sit in seem harmless or maybe just slightly annoying; but what if they are roughly the same seats, whether or not we are on the ground? To rephrase the ancient Greek philosopher Heraclitus, the seat on the plane and the seat in the airport accommodate the same body. The planes we fly in seem like neutral objects, indifferent vessels—until we consider their afterlives and their fragility. Weather may seem like an innocuous, occasionally intrusive background effect to airport hustle and bustle—but it might well include the atmosphere inside the terminal, and climate change wreaked on a global scale, remarked by exhaust smudges behind MD-80s on takeoff.

My friend Mark Yakich once wrote a poem called "Last Flight out of a State of Mind," which starts like this:

> We chose this plane because we didn't know
> It would become the subject
> Of a poem.

Every time we go to the airport to get on a plane we want it to be undramatic, knowing that at any moment the plane could become the subject of scrutiny: a news headline, an unsolved mystery, even just a low-grade logistical debacle. We know something's going on with flight, and yet we often seem caught by surprise.

Airport after airport is specked on the depths of green. The terminals are harlequins.

When the fact of flight does actually become the subject of a poem, as in Michael Earl Craig's recent "What Will I Call This Poem," it is downright shameful, exposing the most frayed ends of air travel:

> I'm sorry, Mom.
> I am a grown man on a plane
> writing about another person's foot.
> My seat will not tip back.

Earlier in the poem as the airplane rumbles across the tarmac and toward the runway, the flight attendant briefs the passengers on safety protocols, to which "not one of us listens. / We are apparently uninterested in this." The airport has become for the speaker of this poem a ground zero of existential tuning in and tuning out, at once.

These two poems suggest that airports are not supposed to be subjects of poems, foci of aesthetic wonder. But curiously, airports are becoming not just centers for dramatic architecture and subjects of poems—airports are also becoming the object of smartphones. A late 2014 magazine ad for Lufthansa shows a couple in a departure gate waiting for their flight, one of them holding out an iPhone to take a self-portrait, airliner and tarmac debris in the background. The focus of this ad is not really the couple, but the couple taking a picture with

The airport becomes a game that conforms only to its own formal rules.

an iPhone. The subject might be said to be the iPhone itself, floating in the foreground—existing, taking part, watching. The ad is for an airline, and therefore ostensibly about *travel*. But these travelers are positioned in the airport, captured and captivated in a moment of waiting—and they are smiling for the camera. The airport terminal is revealed as a mere ambience for the vibrant life of the personal technology, and where the ad's tagline reads "Nonstop you," we might wonder who the "you" in this ad is: Is it the human traveler, or more precisely the boldly pronounced iPhone? And what might it mean to acknowledge and fully embrace this reality, that airports are increasingly geared toward traveling across the smaller landscapes of our handheld screens?

In the book *Aerial Life*, an academic survey of how early air travel construed and imagined the human body, geographer Peter Adey shows how "the aerial body and what it does have become open books to be scrutinized and read" (124). The aerial body for Adey is the human: the pilot, the passenger, the glass-bubble tail gunner—but it is also a body politic, a mass of bodies responding to flight, responding to being in flight, and living with the culture of flight. I take this body to also include airports—these sprawling bodies that become weird katamari balls gathering so many other seemingly unrelated technologies, textures, routines, and habits. In this book I have been trying to

Our deepest insights about airports must—and should—appear as follies.

trace some of the contours of this collective body, the scramble of people and things that converge at airports.

So what has this book been about, finally? I've recorded my own romance with airports, from work to travel, from unexpected aesthetics to unexamined objects. Throughout this book I have been scrutinizing not only the end of airports as such, but how air travel has become insinuated into culture strewn out at large, and into seemingly disparate technologies and far-flung contemporary practices.

The airport is one of many circles, from our scanned thumbprints to our holding patterns, from our life trajectories to eternal returns of gate changes, from the final call for boarding to the moment before the baggage carousel begins to turn. The end of airports is all around us: pulsing, charging, glowing, going, and still going and going, and showing no signs of stopping. This is our terminal.

At the end of airports, all dreams come true.

Bibliography

Adey, Peter. *Aerial Life: Spaces, Mobilities, Affects*. West Sussex: Wiley-Blackwell, 2010.

Augé, Marc. *Non-Places: Introduction to an Anthropology of Supermodernity*. New York: Verso, 1995.

Barthes, Roland. "The Jet-man." *Mythologies*. New York: Noonday, 1957.

Bumiller, Elisabeth. "War Evolves With Drones, Some Tiny as Bugs." *The New York Times*, June 19, 2011.

Craig, Michael Earl. "What Will I Call This Poem." *Talkativeness*. Seattle & New York: Wave Books, 2014.

Davis, Lydia. *Varieties of Disturbance*. New York: Farrar, Strauss and Giroux, 2007.

DeLillo, Don. *Cosmopolis*. New York: Scribner, 2003.

—. "Hammer and Sickle." *The Angel Esmeralda: Nine Stories*. New York: Scribner, 2011.

—. *The Names*. New York: Vintage, 1982.

—. *Underworld*. New York: Scribner, 1997.

—. *White Noise*. New York: Penguin, 1986.

Emerson, Ralph Waldo. "Circles." *Emerson's Essays*. New York: Harper Perennial, 1981.

Fitzgerald, F. Scott. *The Last Tycoon*. New York: Scribner, 1941.

Fuller, Gillian. "Welcome to Windows 2.1: Motion Aesthetics at the Airport." *Politics at the Airport*. Ed. Mark B. Salter. Minneapolis: University of Minnesota Press, 2008.

Gordon, Alastair. *Naked Airport: A Cultural History of the World's Most Revolutionary Structure*. New York: Metropolitan Books, 2004.

Greif, Martin. *The Airport Book: From Landing Field to Modern Terminal.* New York: Mayflower Books, 1979.

Hailey, Arthur. *Airport.* New York: Doubleday, August 1, 2000.

Harrison, Jim. "Sunlight." *Songs of Unreason.* Port Townsend: Copper Canyon Press, 2011.

Hillman, Brenda. "Phone Booth." *The New Yorker*, March 6, 2007.

Houston, Pam. *Contents May Have Shifted.* New York: W.W. Norton & Company, February 6, 2012.

Jameson, Fredric. *Postmodernism, or The Cultural Logic of Late Capitalism.* Durham, NC: Duke University Press, 1990.

Kasarda, John D. and Greg Lindsay. *Aerotropolis: The Way We'll Live Next.* New York: Farrar, Straus and Giroux, 2011.

Lopez, Barry. "Pearyland." *Field Notes: The Grace Note of the Canyon Wren.* New York: Vintage, June 8, 2004.

McFadden, Brian. "The Many Uses of Police Drones." *The New York Times*, May 27, 2012.

Morton, Timothy. *Hyperobjects.* Minneapolis: University of Minnesota Press, November 2013.

Pascoe, David. *Airspaces.* London: Reaktion, 2001.

Scarry, Richard. *A Day at the Airport.* New York: Random House Books for Young Readers, April 24, 2001.

Schaberg, Christopher. *The Textual Life of Airports: Reading the Culture of Flight.* New York: Bloomsbury, 2013.

Schultheis, Rob. "Homage to Faizabad." *Patagonia,* Spring 2001.

Seuss, Dr. *The Cat in the Hat.* New York: Random House, March 12, 1957.

Sommer, Robert. *Tight Spaces: Hard Architecture and How to Humanize It.* Englewood Cliffs: Prentice Hall, 1974.

Stellin, Susan. "Yes! Download that Airport App!" *The New York Times*, February 29, 2012.

Stewart, Kathleen. *Ordinary Affects.* Durham, NC: Duke University Press, 2007.

Tedeschi, Bob. "After the Plane Gets You to the Airport, an App Comes in Handy." *New York Times*, May 2, 2012.

Wallace, David Foster. *Infinite Jest.* New York: Little, Brown & Co., 1996.

—. *The Pale King.* New York: Little, Brown & Co., 2011.

Woolf, Virginia. "The Death of the Moth." *The Death of the Moth and Other Essays*. New York: Harcourt Brace Jovanovich, 1974.

Yakich, Mark. "Last Flight out of a State of Mind." *The Importance of Peeling Potatoes in Ukraine*. New York: Penguin, 2008.

Films

2001: A Space Odyssey. Directed by Stanley Kubrick. MGM, 1968.

Casablanca. Directed by Michael Curtiz. Warner Bros., 1943.

Fight Club. Directed by David Fincher. 20th Century Fox, 1999.

Killing Them Softly. Directed by Andrew Dominik. Plan B Entertainment, 2012.

The Matrix. Directed by Andy Wachowski and Larry Wachowski. Warner Bros., 1999.

Play It Again, Sam. Directed by Herbert Ross. Paramount, 1972.

Punch Drunk Love. Directed by Paul Thomas Anderson. New Line Cinema, 2002.

Up in the Air. Directed by Jason Reitman. Paramount Pictures, 2009.

Web Resources

"Aerobridge Trainees '08." Online video clip. *Youtube*. December 20, 2008. https://www.youtube.com/watch?v=pUAv2CLoDPY (Accessed October 18, 2014.)

AngelaSimmons. "Super. Bored. #Airport. http://mob.li/_PNRoP." May 15, 2012, 12:37 a.m. https://twitter.com/AngelaSimmons/status/202256388506927105 (Accessed October 18, 2014.)

BenRobertson. "Bone dust settled on the unpeopled massage chairs where there was no fire but there was memory of fire. The judge smiled." June 24, 2014, 9:49 a.m. https://twitter.com/BenRobertson/statuses/481448982640472065 (Accessed October 18, 2014.)

"Boeing 737." *Wikipedia*. Last modified October 15, 2014. http://en.wikipedia.org/wiki/Boeing_737 (Accessed October 18, 2014.)

Busch, Simon. "Possibly the World's Most Impressive Paper Plane." *CNN*. February 4, 2014. http://www.cnn.com/2014/02/03/travel/manila-airplane/index.html (Accessed October 18, 2014.)

Drew, Christopher, Jad Mouawad and Matthew L. Wald. "Regulators Around the Globe Ground Boeing 787s." *New York Times*. January 17, 2013. http://www.nytimes.com/2013/01/18/business/regulators-around-the-globe-ground-boeing-787s.html (Accessed October 18, 2014.)

"Drones Transform How America Fights Its Wars." *New York Times*, June 20, 2011. http://www.nytimes.com/slideshow/2011/06/20/world/20110620-DRONES.html (Accessed October 18, 2014.)

Eaton, Kit. "NASA Reveals the Weird and Wonderful Commercial Airliners of 2025." *Fast Company*. January 14, 2011. http://www.fastcompany.com/1717176/nasa-reveals-weird-and-wonderful-commercial-airliners-2025 (Accessed October 18, 2014.)

Emirates website. Venturian Media, 2012. http://www.emirates.com/us/english/flying/our_fleet/emirates_a380/emirates_a380.aspx and http://www.emirates.com/ar/english/plan_book/dubai_international_airport/emirates_terminal_3/emirates_terminal_3.aspx (Accessed October 18, 2014.)

Harrington, Jason Edward. "Dear America, I Saw You Naked." *Politico Magazine*. Published on January 30, 2014. http://www.politico.com/magazine/story/2014/01/tsa-screener-confession-102912_full.html - .VEQsq2YjDXU (Accessed October 18, 2014.)

Herman Miller. Herman Miller Inc., 2012. http://www.hermanmiller.com/Products/Eames-Tandem-Sling-Seating (Accessed October 18, 2014.)

"How Convenient Jetways Helped Kill Airline Glamour." *Deep Glamour*. May 16, 2013. http://www.deepglamour.net/deep_glamour/2013/05/how-convenient-jetways-helped-kill-airline-glamour.html (Accessed October 18, 2014.)

Marana Aerospace Solutions Website. "About Us." Manara Aerospace Solutions, Inc. http://maranaaerospace.com/about-us/ (Accessed October 18, 2014.)

McGeehan, Patrick. "Improving Ground Life for Travelers at Three Airports." *New York Times*. December 7, 2014. http://www.nytimes.com/2014/12/08/nyregion/improving-ground-life-for-travelers-atlaguardia-jfk-and-newark-airports.html (Accessed December 18, 2014.)

Mouawad, Jad. "Fuel Leak is Latest Setback for Boeing 787 Dreamliner." *New York Times*. January 8, 2013. http://www.nytimes.com/2013/01/09/business/fuel-leak-is-latest-setback-for-boeing-787.html (Accessed October 18, 2014.)

OrlandoPBM. "Air Bridge Collapses at Hong Kong Airport, Rips Door Off Cathay A330." *Airnation.net*. April 9, 2013. http://airnation.net/2013/04/07/air-bridge-collapse-hong-kong/ (Accessed October 18, 2014.)

"Parrot AR.Drone Quadricopter Controlled by iPod touch, iPhone, iPad, and Android Devices (Orange/Blue) (Discontinued by Manufacturer)." *Amazon*. September 3, 2010. http://www.amazon.com/Parrot-Quadricopter-Controlled-Discontinued-Manufacturer/dp/B003ZT5HWO (Accessed October 18, 2014.)

Paumgarten, Nick. "Here's Looking at You." *The New Yorker*. May 14, 2012 (print issue). http://www.newyorker.com/magazine/2012/05/14/heres-looking-at-you (Accessed October 18, 2014.)

Pogue, James. "Occupied." *The New Yorker*. May 14, 2012 (print issue). http://www.newyorker.com/magazine/2012/05/14/occupied-3 (Accessed October 18, 2014.)

"Raw Video: Tsunami Wave Strikes Japan Airport." *Associated Press*. Online video clip. *Youtube*. March 11, 2011. https://www.youtube.com/watch?v=6FvJ62qvLBY (Accessed October 18, 2014.)

Rosenbloom, Stephanie. "Test-Flying the 787 Dreamliner." *New York Times* online. November 30, 2012. http://www.nytimes.com/2012/12/02/travel/test-flying-the-boeing-787-dreamliner.html?pagewanted=all&_r=1& (Accessed October 18, 2014.)

Schaberg, Christopher. "Airports." *To the Best of Our Knowledge*. Produced by Doug Gordon. Wisconsin Public Radio and Public Radio International, May 6, 2012. http://www.ttbook.org/book/airports (Accessed October 18, 2014.)

Sharkey, Joe. "Legroom Tight Now? New Seat Is Less Spacious." *New York Times* online. September 21, 2010. http://www.nytimes.com/2010/09/21/business/21road.html (Accessed October 18, 2014.)

"Southwest Airlines Flight 812." *Wikipedia.* Last Modified January 30, 2014. http://en.wikipedia.org/wiki/Southwest_Airlines_Flight_812 (Accessed October 18, 2014.)

vaniped. "Comfort seats while waiting for our flight. Cool. #amsterdam #airport http://instagr.am/p/K4RYuYiLpE/." http://instagr.am/p/K4RYuYiLpE/ (Accessed October 18, 2014.)

Index

Page references for illustrations within text appear in *italics*.